Dog Smiling
Sunday Morning

A Cooking and Reading Experience

The eccentrics, recluses, dreamers, dogs, and children of The Crossing invite you into their little part of the world to celebrate community, life, magic, food, and of course dogs.

Debbie DuPey

Dog Smiling Sunday Morning

DEDICATION

To all dogs.
May they be loved and cherished in the manner they deserve.

Dog Smiling Sunday Morning

TABLE OF CONTENTS

Dog Smiling Sunday Morning

ACKNOWLEDGMENTS

Thank you to the lovely neighbors and friends of The Crossing.
Your names have been changed for your privacy,
but you know who you are.

Thank you Joanie Eppinga, of Eagle Eye Editing
for making me look like I can do grammar.

Thank you Josolynn Jones, for
putting it all together and making it look pretty.

Dog Smiling Sunday Morning

CHAPTER 1

THE CROSSING:
A Perfect Blend of Appetizers to Accompany Any Gathering

The Crossing is a place. It exists. We never call it a little bit of heaven on earth, as there's not a halo to be found for miles around.

We do know we live in a place that is special because of its natural and wild beauty. The pace is a little slower, and we are blessed with a community that was not designed but born. It is common practice in The Crossing to cook meals for the women who have just given birth, assist each other with projects too big to manage, or knock on a door early in the morning in only your pajamas to borrow sugar, eggs, oil, or cream for your coffee. We have our rough edges; we roll our eyes when our neighbors have too many old junked cars parked in front of their house, yell at each other's dogs, and make self-righteous proclamations about the lifestyles and shortcomings of others. But call a potluck, and we're there with our best dishes, hugging and complimenting the same people we criticized that same morning over coffee.

The neighborhood has changed over the years, and not without its share of growing pains. Old hippies built it, and the once carefree tenants are now moving into middle and even old age. Traces of their reckless youth are hinted at in the sarongs they don on summer evenings, but old hippies are not immune to the sourness that sometimes accompanies the golden years; so somewhat reluctantly, the neighborhood has buckled down, shaped up, put its clothes on, and turned its music down.

We've tried to keep a low profile, afraid that once developers find out about our secret neighborhood the world will creep down upon us like a noxious weed. We do have "voyeurs" who, out on a Sunday drive, come upon our little road with its not-so-friendly sign that states: "No River Access. Dead-end." As they turn onto this road with its 60-degree decline, their approach will no doubt scatter the dozen or so half-wild white cats that live at the top of the hill. They may flush out a wild turkey who will take to the air in surprise, letting loose a deep squawk as he leaves the ground. A little herd of quail sunning in the road will frantically form a little parade, and, with heads bopping, make their way to the safety of the underbrush. Magpies will laugh down from low-growing trees.

We're opening up for a moment now. You are our guests. We want to give you a little tour of The Crossing: this place that has attracted so many artists, writers, and recluses to the north bank of the Chinook River.

We are only minutes from downtown, but people who have lived in Chinook all their lives do not know this place. To get here, you must pass through a desolate urban stretch of open grass where the old railway used to run freight trains into downtown Chinook. Also, you must get through the poverty- and crime-stricken neighborhood, often referred to as Felony Flats, that lies just north of the open stretch.

River trails extend east and west of The Crossing. It is a splendid sight to walk along the river and see a heron standing silently, his serrated beak at the ready, his primitive eyes meditating upon the river's water, waiting for fish. Or to see a pair of bald eagles floating on an air current on a blustery day. Squirrels, beaver, marmots, and even a few coyotes are often spotted during ritual morning treks.

The river itself bursts against its banks in spring. It is shaded by deciduous trees that are soft green in spring and roar in fall in all the brighter shades of orange and red. The poison nightshade leaves of three turn to a brilliant crimson for The Crossing's fall.

There is also the nude beach across the way. We tube down the river in the summer, and sometimes flesh in great abundance awaits our eyes as we turn the corner to the beach called People's Park. For decades, the city's nudists have bared their bodies and waded into the chilly waters of the Chinook River with their jewels in full glory. Sometimes the nudists seem to get "lost," and we come upon them strolling along the river, little dongs a-wagging (they're mostly men). Of course, all this is bound to change. But that's later in the story.

Somehow, by some stroke of luck or the will of our own imaginations and passions, we have found ourselves here in these nine houses nestled on a shelf of land just above the banks of the Chinook River. To our east, the buildings of downtown Chinook shine white in the midday sun. We can hear the steeple bells from the Cathedral of Our Lady of Lourdes ringing on the hour when we stand in our yards. To the west is the river trail where we walk among the wild things. In our homes, soups simmer and dogs lie near wood-burning stoves, and on Sunday mornings, these dogs smile.

A Perfect Blend of Appetizers to Begin Any Gathering

This dip and vegetable assortment is just complicated enough to make your guests think you're amazing, but simple enough so you won't be crying over a hot stove 15 minutes before your guests arrive, and finally give up and fall to your backup plan: Cheese Whiz on Ritz crackers.

Hummus with flavor options & Baba Ghanoush

Serve with olives, crackers or bread, vegetables and cheeses.

Hummus – *with flavor options*

Ingredients:

- 2 14-oz cans garbanzo beans, drained
- Juice of 2 lemons
- 2 garlic cloves, chopped
- 3 tablespoons olive oil
- 1 teaspoon cayenne pepper
- ⅔ cup tahini paste
- Paprika to taste

Additional flavor options:

- ¼ cup roasted red peppers – reserve a few slivers for decoration
- ¼ cup artichoke hearts – reserve one sliver for decoration
- ¼ cup Kalamata olives – reserve one olive for decoration

Instructions:

1. Place the garbanzo beans and garlic in a food processor and blend until smooth.
2. Add the lemon juice, garlic, olive oil, cayenne pepper, and tahini and blend until creamy.
3. Separate the hummus into four portions (One will stay in this form, so you can put it in the bowl of your choosing.).
4. Place one of the portions back in the food processor and blend.
5. Repeat with other two flavor options, cleaning the food processor between options to avoid mixing the flavors.
6. Top with an additional drizzle of olive oil, ground black pepper, and a sprinkle of paprika.
7. Decorate the flavor options with their respective ingredient.

Baba Ghanoush – *like hummus except with eggplant*

Ingredients:

- 2 medium eggplants
- 2 tablespoons tahini
- 2 garlic cloves, chopped
- Juice of 1 lemon
- Sprinkle of salt
- ¼ cup plain yogurt

Instructions:

1. Preheat oven to 400 degrees F.
2. Roast eggplants in the oven for about 1 hour, until their skin darkens, and the flesh feels soft. For a smoky flavor, eggplant can be sliced in half and roasted on a BBQ grill for about ½ hour.
3. Let eggplants cool, and then split them in the center and scoop out the flesh. Place flesh in food processor, add remaining ingredients **except yogurt**, and blend until smooth. Blend yogurt in immediately before serving.

CHAPTER 2

TRIBAL KINSHIPS:
Salads

The Crossing has its crossroads. As at all crossroads, magical things happen here. Well, mostly we just sort of congregate near the crossroads on summer mornings in our pajamas, coffee cups in hands, gossiping and admiring each other's children and laughing about our dogs. And there is plenty to gossip about. The connections and mischief of those who live here is always a fantastic subject.

First, some introductions. When you get to the bottom of hill, you pass a slight kink in the road before it straightens and heads due west in the same path as the river. This is Water Ave.

If you stay to the left, you're on Crossing Street. The Crossing is where the ferry used to run, connecting the North Side folks to the South Side folks before the turn of the century. This little community sprang up essentially as a ferry community. At one time it had double the current number of houses.

Only two houses remain from early settlements on Crossing Street. At the end, an old house of fine wood and stone looks out over the river. The house's owner, Gus, is our resident doctor. He treats our poison ivy and hand slivers. Gus is soap-opera-doctor handsome, complete with a Dr. Zhivago moustache. He studies Buddhism and is fascinated by mushrooms. Somewhere in The Crossing, enormous Elephant Ear mushrooms grow wild. Gus guards their secret location with diligence.

Gus's property extends north to a large lot where he has arranged an impressive garden of granite. Next to this is the little white rental house on the corner. The residents here rotate every few years. Right now, a young artist named Ethan keeps strange hours and has a rusty old bedspring on his back deck that he seems to be fashioning into a sculpture.

Across from Ethan's is Concetta's cedar-plank cottage that's perched on a slight embankment, so you have to climb up little steps to get to her front door. Odd found objects adorn her overgrown yard. A real stuffed crow lurks in the branches of a tree. A cowboy boot has become birdfeeder. A wrought-iron headboard stands as a gate to a flowerbed. Concetta is a potter who shapes clay into soul-inspired forms that tell her stories of grief, love, and laughter.

The south side of the street hosts the main row of houses, beginning with Lydia's house, which is really more of a commune than a single-resident home. The "arrangements" of this household are one of our favorite sources of gossip. Lydia's salmon-colored home has numerous odd-shaped add-ons to accommodate her two raven-haired daughters, Caitlin and Nicole, an ex-husband, Billy, and one of Billy's four other ex-wives.

Lydia's large yard has beautiful, well-tended flowerbeds: an assortment of lilies, perennials, and annuals she constantly updates. Rosebushes and dahlias surround birdbaths, stepping-stones create walking paths, and behind the house, a wide deck provides a sweeping view of the river. It is appropriate that Lydia has a yard of such grandeur; she is, after all, the self-proclaimed mayor of The Crossing.

Almost everything and everybody in The Crossing can be traced back to Billy—our handyman. Currently, as I mentioned, he lives with Lydia and one of his other ex-wives, Kathy. But he really just lives everywhere.

Billy has left his mark throughout the neighborhood, through children he's fathered, women he's loved, and houses he's remodeled. Because of his usefulness and charm, women seem to take care of him. A Hawaiian Japanese man who still looks thirty even though he's in his mid-sixties, he goes barefoot in summer and flirts without discretion with all the women of The Crossing. Appearing at my door with a kitchen faucet to replace my old leaky one, he strokes its voluptuous curves: "It's very feminine, don't you think?" he asks me, his chocolate eyes twinkling mischievously.

Billy has seduced and nurtured the whole neighborhood landscape through his sensuous eye and crafty hands. He is credited with having created most of The Crossing's unique charm: the picket fences with their angled tops, an assortment of cairns, and especially the wild Japanese knotweed that he brought in from somewhere that looks much like bamboo but grows more profusely and is far less manageable. These upward-bound green stalks that we sometimes refer to as "Billy's penises" sprout up in our yards and flowerbeds to form little Asian-style groves all around The Crossing.

I live in the next house, with my son, Marcus. It's large and dark, cobbled together into cumbersome spaces that are almost unlivable. I rent the house from Brenda, who left The Crossing with a broken heart fourteen years ago when her marriage fell apart. She's anxiously trying to find a man to move back here with her, a man with a chainsaw and a truck. Despite this house's dilapidation and awkward layout, I am happy to have been able to raise my son within its walls. It's been safe and warm.

West of me live Hank and Morgan and their triplets: Nathan, Cody, and Tanner. The triplets tumbled into the neighborhood like a handful of marbles five years ago and delight us all with their numerous antics. Stomping about with nude bottoms and mismatched plastic boots, they make the rest of us, with our matching shoes, seem quite dull. They color with crayons on walls. A reasonable living-room arrangement has been replaced with a concoction of climbing toys and makeshift sheet tents. A large-screen TV beams cartoons almost constantly. The triplets have strained Hank and Morgan's relationship. This comes up at the crossroads. Is Hank moving out, or will they just remodel again? Maybe another family excursion to the Oregon Coast?

The neatest, and by "neat" I mean the house seems to have been constructed using an actual layout and has paint trim that makes sense, belongs to Lisa and John and their kids. The whole family seems sprung from the pages of Sunset Magazine. You can imagine them in a glossy photo on their back deck overlooking the river, all big smiles and blonde hair. Lisa's son from a previous marriage, Leonard, is one of our neighborhood's precious people. Stricken with cerebral palsy, and locked into a mind of an infant, he is cared for with great tenderness by these beautiful and kind people.

We miss the man who lived in the tall and narrow burnt-orange house adjacent to John and Lisa's place. His name was Joe. He was friendly but not too loud. His prolific tomato plants grew along the street, and he would offer these juicy red globes up to me when I walked by during late summer. But then he sold his home to this rather odd, unfriendly woman who sings opera and who complains about our free-range dogs.

When we gather outside in summer for an early evening barbeque, strains of Bolero accost our ears.

"She must be crazy," we whisper at the crossroads. "I wish she'd just move out."

Ralph lives in the last and most dilapidated house of The Crossing, a monstrous green structure teetering on the hill above the river and flanked by a wild bank of land to the west.

Ralph is a recluse.

Once a young man from across the river saw Ralph's house and thought he needed help. He decided to be a Good Samaritan. He rode his bike into The Crossing just as Hank was loading the triplets in the V-bus. The young man stopped to confirm that he was heading in the direction of the big green house where that poor old man lived. Before Hank could get the triplets buckled into their car seats, the young man was coming back on his bike, looking a bit ruffled.

"He said he was going to shoot me if I didn't get off his porch!"

All I've ever seen of Ralph is his large head covered in a froth of white hair and beard as he drives his van through The Crossing.

The neighborhood is on an edge: the edge of the river, the edge of the city. You could say the people here live on edges as well: the edges of sanity, reason, creativity, society, stability. We feel protected on this shelf of land, like a lost tribe that has found haven away from the elements and society's abrasive intrusions.

This connects us! We are the tribe of The Crossing.

Salads

The secret to creating a good salad is really in making sure it looks pretty. This is true. Your eyes take in the information for the brain and then the brain tells the taste buds that something really yummy is coming their way. You've won them over without taking a bite. There is some sort of weird mojo around color, too. If the colors are a nice mix, then it's going to taste good. More color. More flavor. I don't care if science does or does not prove this. I believe it, and therefore it's true to me.

If you believe, you can prepare salads with confidence. Just by looking at the ingredients spread out on the counter, you'll know what your salad needs: not more tart, smoky, sweet, or salty, but more green, more red, more yellow. Oh, and then there is the texture palette complimenting the color palette: velvety, cool, pebbly, dry, wet, and the 100 different kinds of crunchy: nut crunchy, cool, juicy crunchy, dry crouton crunchy. Expand your salad vocabulary and you'll never experience salads the same again. Be bold and plunge into the spectacular jungles of flavor variety found in your produce and condiment aisles.

Mixed Green Salad with Grilled Chicken and Blue Cheese

- 4 cups assorted spring greens
- 1 slivered red pepper
- 2 chicken breasts, drizzled with 2 tablespoons soy sauce and 1 tablespoon sweet molasses, 1 tablespoon chopped fresh garlic, 1 tablespoon olive oil, and salt and pepper. Grilled or broiled about 20 minutes until done in center and sliced into bite-size pieces.
- ¼ cup chopped green olives
- ¼ cup blue cheese
- 4 tablespoons virgin olive oil
- 3 tablespoons balsamic vinegar
- 2 cloves garlic, finely minced
- Salt and freshly ground black pepper to taste

Instructions:

1. Mix spring greens with olive oil, garlic, and balsamic vinegar.
2. Arrange chicken pieces, olives, red pepper slices, and blue cheese on top of greens.
3. Add salt and pepper to taste.

Mediterranean Summer Salad

- 1 cup finely chopped fresh basil
- 1 cup torn spinach leaves
- ½ cup artichoke hearts
- ½ cup Kalamata olives, sliced
- 4 vine-ripened tomatoes, chopped
- 1 cucumber, sliced
- ½ cup cooked pasta (optional – for a heartier salad)
- ½ cup crumbled feta cheese
- Juice of two lemons
- Freshly ground pepper
- Salt to taste

Instructions:

1. Mix herbs with tomatoes, sliced cucumber, and feta cheese.
2. Sprinkle with lemon juice.
3. Toss lightly and add salt and ground pepper to taste.

Spring Asparagus Salad
with Almond Couscous

- 3 cups fresh asparagus, lightly steamed and cut into 3-inch lengths
- ⅔ cup uncooked couscous
- 1 cup water
- ½ cup yogurt
- ¼ cup virgin olive oil
- 1 tablespoon tahini
- 2 teaspoons ground ginger
- 1 teaspoon cumin
- ¼ cup mixture of lemon and orange juice
- ¼ cup golden raisins
- ½ cup slivered almonds
- ¼ cup combination of oregano and cilantro

Instructions:

1. Bring water to a boil and add couscous, return to a boil, and remove from heat.
2. Cover with a lid and let sit for 5 minutes.
3. Mix yogurt, olive oil, tahini, ginger, and cumin.
4. Mix with couscous in large bowl.
5. Toss in steamed asparagus, raisins, oregano, almonds, cilantro, and citrus juice.
6. Chill for 1–2 hours and serve.

CHAPTER 3

THE DOGS OF THE CROSSING:
Treats for Your Best Friend

The dogs of The Crossing smile on Sunday mornings. Actually, they smile every day. If there is any true happiness in The Crossing, it belongs to the dogs. The people leave in the morning for the drudgery of the real world—clients, time clocks, students, appointments, and classes. The dogs see us off lovingly from the driveway. "I'll be good," their long, sloping tails seem to wag. "I'll take care of things while you're gone," their sincere looks reassure us. "Come back soon!"

And then, well, we suspect the dogs have pretty dynamic social lives once we leave and their day begins. It is an open range in our neighborhood. A great deal of the dogs' time is spent sunning themselves in the middle of street. When a car comes down the road, they look up at it begrudgingly. The car must stop as the dogs slowly pull themselves up from the pavement and walk in a leisurely manner to the side of the road. My dog Jubilee sometimes gets up from her post in the road's center and wanders over to Concetta's house. This is also where Scully lives.

Jubilee picks up Scully's dog-food-filled dish in her mouth and carries it back to our yard. She lies in the tall grass and nibbles. Scully sulks on her porch, not having the nerve to hold her ground against my she-bully husky.

The dogs' day usually begins at the house of Lydia, the unofficial mayor of The Crossing. Lydia starts her own day with a morning walk along the river. With pockets full of dog treats, she heads out of her fenced yard, followed by her two dogs, Marengo and Billy. Yes, she seems to have named one of her dogs after the ex-husband who continues to reside with her. She swears it wasn't intentional: "He just looks like a Billy."

The other dogs meet her in the street for their daily morning snack, one of many to come as the day progresses. They even have the mailman and the meter reader trained to deliver them snacks on their rounds.

Rocket, the lanky golden retriever-Lab mix, will lope along behind Lydia on her walk. Jubilee will not leave the neighborhood and abandon her watch. Scully is a wild card. Maybe she'll stay; maybe she'll go. Mostly Scully will choose whatever situation is most likely to yield a game of fetch. She's one of those compulsive retriever types.

Lydia seems to like dogs more than she does people. She is a tall, angled woman with a regal mass of curly red hair crowning a very Roman profile. Her sharp blue eyes scan for information as she walks the neighborhood surrounded by her pack of dogs. "Who is that man on Concetta's porch? What the hell is Gus building now? I wish I could take a weed whacker to that mess of weeds in their yard."

Marengo, a pitbull mix, was discovered by Lydia about ten years ago. Lydia found her up in the desolate area above us where the old train tracks used to run. Marengo was skinny and wild, living off marmots, which she hunted down with the savagery of a hyena. Though she's been tamed by Lydia, it is wise to call her name before entering her domain. When she comes at you full throttle, teeth exposed and barking ferociously, you wonder if she remembers that only yesterday you were petting her head and if she ever longs to sink her teeth into something living, as she did in the wild days of her youth.

Billy is another of Lydia's orphans. He's a miniature collie whose mellow and kind disposition is in stark contrast to Marengo's fierce demeanor. Lydia shaves him in summer when it gets too hot and his fur starts to mat. It's not a very becoming look for poor Billy. In fact, he looks more miniature anteater than collie.

Lydia writes anonymous letters to neglectful dog owners in Felony Flats, the crime-plagued area right above The Crossing. In broad daylight she marches to their back doors and tapes the notes where they are sure to find them upon returning home after their hard day's work.

"I'm your dog," the letter proclaims. "Why do you leave me outside all day tied to this chain? All I want is to be loved."

Rocket belongs to Hank and Morgan, but since the arrival of their triplets, he has been having sleepovers at other dogs' houses, where he gets more attention. Pre-triplets Rocket truly fit his name. Bounding over fences, he seemed more gazelle than dog. He was a nuisance. He used to steal my wooden porch "art." I called it art, though no one else probably saw the pieces of driftwood I'd collected on the Oregon coast that way. Rocket dragged all my wooden treasures over to his yard, where he gnawed the wave-twisted driftwood into fetching sticks. He dug holes in all our yards. When we drove through The Crossing, he loped dangerously near the front wheels of our cars. At the crossroads, we would mutter, "We need to do something about that dog." Even by Crossing standards, he was undisciplined.

Postpartum Rocket, on the other hand, is depressed. His house has been taken over, first by screaming babies and then by the troublesome toddlers they became. His ragged, sleep-deprived owners have no time for him. Now he mopes around the neighborhood with a drooping head, his spirit crushed. Rocket goes from house to house with sad, wrinkled eyes, his boyhood luster gone. He spends a great deal of time with Gus, Shawn, and Gus's big shepherd, Zoë. Rocket often spends the night in Gus's house, even sleeping in the bed where Gus's ex-wife used to sleep.

"It seems unhygienic," we shrug while gathered at the crossroads.

Ralph's dog Maui used to live in The Crossing, but now it seems he's dead. We haven't seen him in a couple of years. It was painful to watch him hobble down Falls Ave. with his arthritic legs and ulcered skin, his red hair matted around big fatty tumors. Legend has it he also might just be a little burned out from having marijuana hits blown into his face while visiting Lydia's hippie parties.

He had one great moment of passion in his elderly days, after my son, Marcus, adopted a prissy and hyper little dachshund named Tasha that he dressed in a sweater and adorned with a spiked collar. One day Tasha pranced about the neighborhood provocatively with her slender tail especially rigid: she was in heat.

The fire of her instinctual procreative urge penetrated through to even Maui's dulled senses. He made his way down Falls Street, despite the midday sun and his many maladies. For a moment, he was but a strutting young pup. He bobbed his graying head curiously and even mustered up a little bounce in his walk. He sniffed about Tasha's firm little body, and there seemed to be a little sparkle coming from his usually faded eyes. Feeling that it just wasn't right to allow this mangy old dog to have his way with this sweet young thing, Marcus ushered Tasha and her frantically wagging tail into the house. Poor defeated Maui slowly made his way back to his saggy porch and the dish of generic dog food and waited out his last days.

A dog's life, even in The Crossing, has its sorrows.

The dogs of The Crossing become legendary after death. That was especially the case with Nose. Nose passed away nearly fifteen years ago. Nose was deaf and blind. He belonged to Lydia, Billy, and their girls, Shalia and Megan. Billy the handyman wrote a series of children's books in which Nose accomplishes great feats and even does a little bit of yoga.

Our Doctor Gus believes his deceased dog Clovis, a terrier-type dog with a corkscrew tail, had Buddha spirit. Clovis maintained a special peace with all the other dogs of the neighborhood. Gus imitates the manner in which his dog sniffed the air and meditated on his surroundings. "One day I said, 'Clovis, you want to ride?' Clovis began to run toward the truck and then just fell over dead. I cried for weeks."

Gus has built a shrine where Clovis is buried. A figurine of a fawn adorns the grave, and a statue of St. Frances of Assisi, saint of animals, gazes kindly downward. One hand extends out to all the dogs in The Crossing.

Doggie Treats

- 2 cups flour (You have the option of using 1 cup white flour and 1 cup whole wheat or 2 cups white flour)
- ½ cup xylitol-free peanut butter
- 2 eggs

Instructions:

1. Mix these three ingredients in a bowl, adding water sparingly until it reaches a consistency where the dough can be rolled.
2. Place the dough on parchment paper so it isn't quite so messy.
3. Use cookie cutters.
4. Place on an uncreased cookie sheet.
5. Bake for 20 minutes at 350 degrees F.

CHAPTER 4

AN INTERVIEW WITH THE MAYOR OF THE CROSSING:
Hippie Recipes

In the early '70s, Lydia dreamed of buying a sweet farmhouse on the golden mounds of land in Valleyford. When her dream house was bought out from under her nose, she sulked. It was a tight market. This single hippie gal working part time in a bookstore didn't have a lot of money to compete.

"Have you ever considered living in The Crossing?" a friend asked. Lydia had never heard of the place. "I want to live in the country, not in town," Lydia clarified. But her friend took her down to show her this place in the city that was not really citified at all.

"This is nasty!" Lydia scowled, looking at the mess of falling-down, garbage-riddled houses and the abandoned cars littering the neighborhood. "Why would I want to live down here in this junky place?" she asked her friend.

A few months later, on an impulse, she went back down to The Crossing. She saw a For Sale sign in front of a burned-down house. Eight dead cars were lined up bumper to bumper beneath the limbs of an old dead apple tree. The only promising aspect of the

19

place was a beehive with bees hovering around.

Lydia scribbled down the number from the faded sign and thought, I'll just call and see what is for sale. Maybe it was the beehive or the old wringer washer.

It turned out the whole house was for sale.

"How much?" Lydia inquired.

"Fifty-five," said the family representative.

"Fifty-five thousand?"

"Fifty-five hundred!"

Lydia froze, considering the plot of land above the river. It was an opportunity to have a real place of her own. The original owners had died and left it to their son, who accidentally burned the place down. The house and land were only a nuisance to the remaining family.

So, for fifty-five hundred dollars, Lydia became the owner of the six junk-cluttered, overgrown lots. The property came with a beehive, three fruit trees, a wringer washer, two ponies, eight cars, a rusted-out bus, and a burned-out house.

The upside was that from where she stood from her back porch, she had a magnificent view of the river. The water beneath was shallow, and round river rocks peeked through the surface. It looked amazing straight, and even better when she was a wee bit stoned on Mary Jane. (Again, it was the '70s.)

At the time, the neighborhood was filled with the motliest of residents. In the old ferry crosser's house, now Gus's, about ten hippies lived with an equal number of pigmy goats and numerous dogs, cats, and chickens that roamed, ate, and peed and pooped freely about the yard and inside the house. There was Don Riddle, with his masses of collectibles piled so high that his house was nearly indistinguishable from the surrounding trash. Everywhere, he had mounds of metal and scrap lumber, discarded furniture, sinks, toilets, bedsprings, and more. Across the street from Don was the "cat lady," so called because of the dozens of stray cats she kept. Daily she wandered about the neighborhood, a cigarette hanging from her mouth, yelling at some ghost man, "Goddamn son-of-a-bitch!"

An old lady named Pearl lived in what for years was referred to as "the pink house." Other houses staggered along the area we call "the Habitat," which was then called East Crossing. Here lived the real ne'er-do-wells, essentially squatters who just set up homes in these abandoned houses.

"I just dropped out when I moved down here!" Lydia explains. "Me and my boyfriend at the time totally gutted the house and remodeled it. Not in a refined sort of way, but we made it livable."

There were a whole lot of hippies and freaks and geeks who migrated in and out. Lydia didn't care, because it was the '70s, and this was what being alternative was all about. Partiers came and lived for a while. Lovers came and went, or more often she threw them out.

One of the guys who kept showing up at the parties was Billy. Pictures from this time show him, gazelle-like, leaping across the river, or standing wide-eyed next to a sunflower, lean and naked, grinning happily. There are also pictures of Lydia, angular and with ruffled hair, showing off big barrels filled with ripe red tomatoes, or sitting among the wildflowers that dappled her yard in sprays of blues, reds, and yellows.

"One day the cops drove by," Lydia says. "I realized I had a whole shed filled with marijuana—150 kilos." Lydia wasn't really involved with selling drugs, but when her friends needed a place to store their pot supply, she didn't see any harm in giving them the use of her shed. "When I saw the cops come down, I realized I could go to jail."

It was time to clean house. She shooed everyone away. "It was 'out! Out! All of you, out!'"

By then, the Hawaiian guy named Billy had settled in. Pretty soon their daughter Caitlin was born, followed by Nicole. Both were born right in Lydia's bedroom with the help of a midwife, surrounded by friends and comforted by the river waters.

Through these years, the neighborhood changed. Lydia's smart and tender stewardship of the neighborhood guided this change. She brought a better class of hippie to The Crossing, people who kept their goats out of their houses and tended to their vegetable gardens.

Lydia slowly replaced her wild hippie garden with a rather stately collection of well-organized flowerbeds.

In the early 1970s, The Crossing was the armpit of Chinook. Today, the neighborhood is no longer "nasty." Today, it is sweetly eccentric.

Lydia attends city hall meetings and forums to keep her finger on the pulse of what "those bureaucrats" might be planning that could affect her little river community. Some, I'm sure, consider her a crotchety busybody. I smile at this, because I've seen pictures of Lydia the free spirit sitting along the river like a naked and beautiful river nymph.

It feels as if it's only through Lydia's good graces that we are allowed to be part of the community. She is the Chieftain-mayor of this tribe at The Crossing. It's a good idea to bring her food offerings. Bring your sarong. You might be inspired to lose your inhibitions and do your own hippie dance on the river's sandy bank.

Hippie Recipes

Spaghetti Squash and Fresh Vegetable Toss

& The Original Vegetarian Hippie Sandwich

Spaghetti Squash and Fresh Vegetable Toss

Ingredients:
- 1 medium-size spaghetti squash
- 1 tablespoon olive oil

- 2 cups lightly steamed broccoli florets
- 1 cup shredded carrots
- 1 cup chopped green onions
- ½ cube butter
- ¼ cup parmesan cheese
- 2 tablespoons virgin olive oil
- 1 tablespoon chili pepper flakes
- Salt and pepper to taste
- 1 cup mixed fresh herbs, such as dill, basil, oregano, parsley

Instructions:

1. Preheat oven to 425 degrees F.
2. Cut spaghetti squash in half and remove innards. Rub with olive oil and bake for 20 minutes.
3. Remove squash meat with a large spoon and place in a large bowl. Separate strands as much as possible. Melt butter on hot squash and add olive oil, vegetables, and herbs and parmesan cheese. Toss gently and serve while still hot.

The Original Vegetarian Hippie Sandwich

Ingredients:

- Thick slices of whole-grain bread
- Sharp cheddar cheese slices
- Tomato slices
- Alfalfa or other sprouts
- Avocado
- Mayonnaise and mustard
- Cumin, salt, and red chili (optional)
- Lime slice (optional)

(It is a matter of taste if you want to keep your avocado in slices or make into an avocado spread. If you want to do the avocado spread, then mash the avocado and add cumin and red chili and a dash of lime juice.)

Spread mayonnaise on one piece of whole-grain bread and mustard on the other piece. If using the avocado spread, then place a generous layer of spread on the piece of bread with mayonnaise. Layer in this order: cheese slices, tomatoes, avocado, and sprouts. Top with second bread slice. Cut in half and enjoy the simplistic but beautifully complementary flavor combination of this rustic sandwich.

CHAPTER 5

HOW TO FIND A HOME:
Soups to Nourish the Heart!

Recalling your touch
My flower petals blush
Dawn comes in blossom!

There are two kinds of prayers: "Please, please, please" and "Thank you! Thank you! Thank you!"

When the heart reaches out with sincerity and pain, like flowers seeking sunshine, the first prayer evokes the second.

We all came to The Crossing in our own manner. Lisa followed her cousin Lydia. Gus was drawn here because one day he followed an eagle flying along the river. Concetta came here to recover from a broken heart.

Concetta has had her lovers. Good-hearted men who wooed her with compliments about her cute little nose and flirty black curls. Men who were intrigued by her need for artistic expression and her lack of convention. Men who tried to save her from adventures when she attempted to live out a vagabond fantasy of living in a chrome travel trailer, roaming about the U.S. with her dog and girls and paintbrushes. She's had a rich publisher boyfriend from New York, a poor cowboy, and a jazz musician. They came in a full spectrum of ethnicities, religions, colors, and political persuasions. Her love repertoire was unbiased. The only thing the men ever had in common was that they were all tall. Very, very tall.

And then it happened. The one love that made Concetta pull up the drawbridge. What can I say about him without sounding trite? He was everything you would expect him to be. Beautiful and broken. The kind of man that makes a woman's breast ache, it longs so to nurture and heal. So Concetta the artist, the independent spirit, hunkered down to fix her man. His name was Jack, and he was six foot five inches tall. Very, very tall!

There was a quality about the two of them, an understanding that was immediate, because, like Jack, Concetta had her childhood of pain and abandonment: an alcoholic dad and childhood homes where voices yelled and souls shrank. So much was understood without words. Jack never asked anything of Concetta but that she accept him for who he was, complete with all those fragmented pieces, sharp edges, and hurtful behaviors. But after ten years of his broken ways of being, Concetta's heart grew tired.

One day, when Concetta came down to The Crossing to visit Lydia, Lydia told her to go look at the house across the street, once owned by "the cat woman" but being remodeled for resale by Billy.

Perhaps it was while standing on the porch that Concetta realized she could not heal Jack, could not keep him out of other women's beds or sober in the morning. Perhaps the river's water called home her own tears.

She experienced a moment of peace standing on the porch, looking out over the squat neighborhood houses peeking out through overgrown shrubs. Her spirit settled. "This is my home!" she declared to Billy. "I'm going to live here!" It was a moment of clarity. In this house, with its many windows that let in the sun, she knew the chaos and sadness she had fallen into would recede.

Concetta picked up a rock from the front yard, and for over a year she carried it in her pocket. Buried in debt and with only a part-time job, she didn't know how she could buy the house, but she knew she would. As the year passed, she carried the rock and continued to pray. "Please God, please."

In that year, her father grew sick. The same year, her mother's mind gave in to senility. Concetta spent her time tending ill parents and mothering her two daughters. When her father died, he left Concetta just enough money to buy the house. In her pocket was the rock she had carried for eighteen months.

Now she lives alone. Jack's old truck is parked, abandoned, in her back driveway. He also left a bicycle, and an old red cruiser from the '60s is in her shed.

From my porch, I see Concetta in her garden, pulling weeds. Her body arches gracefully as if forged from a combination of sadness and strength. She has a studio behind her house. Here she creates sculptures with such mundane but profound titles as "16 Steps to Fall Asleep!" Now she's got a vision in her head, something that brings in the skeletons of real, once-live birds. The neighbors have become like cats and are dropping dead birds off at her house like little prizes. She puts them in her freezer and giggles at the morbid nature of her art.

"Something about flight and angels," she says, and shrugs.

Each Christmas, she throws a party. Her small house fills with neighbors, friends, and family. Together, we sing Christmas carols and whisper and laugh. She makes soup. "This is my thank-you to The Crossing for taking me in."

"There's a lot of pain in life. But there is so much more to celebrate."

Your gentle night heart
Bird fluttering sad thunder
Beneath my hand, hush!

Soups to Nourish the Heart!

Any one of these soups may cure a broken heart. Once a friend of mine was so broken-hearted that she hadn't eaten for days. I took her down on my deck overlooking the river. In the afternoon sunlight, she shared the story of the handsome man who didn't call her back. I didn't respond with an "I'm so sorry!" or "That bastard! How could he?" I just gave her a hug and said, "Let me bring you some soup." After the first bowl, you could see her start to perk up. Later that week she came to a party with a new and just as handsome man. They were all smiles. I've got the soup on the back burner just in case. Love is too fickle to not always be prepared.

Soups:
- Butternut Squash Soup with Homemade Croutons and Parmesan Cheese
- Chicken-Tomatillo Soup
- Brazilian Vatapa with Cod
- Mediterranean Bean and Olive Soup

Butternut Squash Soup with Homemade Croutons and Parmesan Cheese

- 1¾ pounds squash, peeled and seeded and cut into 1-inch cubes – approx. 6 cups
- 3 tablespoons olive oil
- 3 teaspoons salt
- 2 teaspoons freshly ground black pepper
- 1 tablespoon butter
- 1 large onion, diced
- 3 celery stalks, chopped
- 6 cups vegetable broth
- 1 tablespoon fresh sage, chopped
- 2 tablespoons chopped chives
- Dollop of plain Greek yogurt
- ½ cup grated Parmesan cheese
- Paprika to taste

For croutons
- 4 slices herbed rustic bread, torn into large chunks
- 3 tablespoons olive oil

Instructions:
1. Toss bread chunks in olive oil, spread on a baking sheet, and toast for 10 minutes or until golden brown. Set aside.
2. Mix squash with olive oil and place on a baking sheet and bake at 400 degrees F for 20 minutes; turn over and bake another 15.
3. In a large stockpot, heat the butter.
4. Add the onion, celery, and sage and sauté over medium heat until the vegetables are translucent, about 10 minutes.

5. Add the squash, broth, salt, and pepper.
6. Lower the heat and let simmer for 30 minutes.
7. Using a blender or food processor, blend the soup in batches until smooth. Soup can be returned to pot to keep warm.
8. Serve in bowls with a small dollop of sour cream, a sprinkling of Parmesan cheese, a dash of paprika, and two or three homemade croutons.

Chicken- Tomatillo Soup

- 1½ tablespoons olive oil
- ½ onion, finely minced
- 6 cloves garlic
- 2 chicken breasts
- 3 celery stalks, chopped
- 2 teaspoons crushed chilies
- 2 teaspoons ground cumin
- 1 tablespoon paprika
- 8 cups chicken broth
- 20 tomatillos, husks removed, quartered
- 1 4-oz can of tomato paste
- 2 cups fresh or frozen corn
- 1 tablespoon honey
- 1 tablespoon vinegar
- 1 4-oz can mild chilies, chopped.
- 1 whole chicken breast still on the bone
- Salt and pepper to taste
- ½ cup fresh cilantro, cleaned and minced
- Avocado slices
- Sour cream

Instructions:

1. In a large soup pot, heat the olive oil and add the onion, celery, and crushed peppers. Sauté for 5 minutes.
2. Stir in the cumin and paprika; add the stock, tomatillos, tomato paste, corn, honey, green chilies, and the chicken breast.
3. Simmer until the breast is cooked through, about 15 minutes.

4. Using a slotted spoon, remove the breast. Let broth simmer while breast cools enough to be handled. Bone and skin the cooled breast; then shred the meat. Add the shredded chicken to the soup and season with salt and pepper.
5. After it's served into bowls, sprinkle with fresh cilantro and add salt and pepper to taste.

Brazilian Vatapa with Cod

- 1 lb cod, cut into 1-inch chunks
- 3 tablespoons oil
- 1 large onion, finely chopped
- 3 cloves garlic
- 1 tablespoon grated fresh ginger
- 3 small jalapeno chilies, seeded and finely chopped
- 5 tomatoes, peeled, seeded, and coarsely chopped
- Juice of 2 limes
- ⅓ cup peanut butter
- 1 cup vegetable or chicken broth
- 1 cup beer
- 2 cups coconut milk
- Tabasco sauce to taste
- 1 teaspoon salt
- 1 cup cilantro, chopped
- 2 limes, cut into wedges

Instructions:

1. In a soup pot, sauté onion, garlic, and ginger over medium-low heat for 10 minutes.
2. Add the tomatoes and peanut butter; stir together for 1 minute more.
3. Begin slowly stirring in the chicken stock while continuing to stir so that the mixture becomes smooth.
4. Add the beer and coconut milk, cilantro, salt, and Tabasco sauce and the cod pieces.
5. Simmer for 6–8 minutes.
6. Serve in large bowls, accompanied with rice. Squeeze a lime wedge over each bowl.

Mediterranean Bean and Olive Soup

- 2 8-oz cans of your favorite white beans
- 3 teaspoons olive oil
- 1 medium onion, diced
- 3 cloves garlic, minced
- 2 stalks of celery, minced
- 1 carrot, minced
- 1 red and one green pepper, minced
- 1 14-oz can stewed tomatoes
- ¼ cup red wine
- 2 cups chicken or vegetable broth
- 2 cups water
- 2 small zucchinis, chopped.
- 1 cup sliced and pitted mixed black and green olives
- 3 tablespoons fresh oregano, chopped
- 1 tablespoon fresh thyme, chopped
- 2 tablespoons fresh basil
- ¼ cup chopped parsley
- Salt and pepper
- Splash of red wine vinegar

Instructions:

1. Heat oil in a soup pan. Sauté onion and garlic for 5 minutes, until translucent.
2. Add celery, carrot, and bell pepper. Sauté another 5 minutes.
3. Add tomatoes; stir and cook for another 5 minutes.
4. Add broth and beans and allow to simmer for 1 minute.
5. Add wine, oregano, thyme, and basil and continue simmering for ½ hour.
6. Add zucchini and parsley; let simmer for 5 more minutes.
7. Add a splash of red wine vinegar and salt and pepper to taste.

CHAPTER 6

MIDNIGHT VOODOO:
Gumbo Z'Herbs

I love how deep longings possess people. I love the poetry and pathology of their manifestations, the vulnerabilities they cause to erupt from deep within. Darcy is a person with longings. What she longed for most of all was a home in The Crossing.

An amazingly strong and agile athlete, competitive, solitary, dog-loving, and intelligent, Darcy came to The Crossing weekly, but not as a tourist—more like a ghost wanting in. With her dogs, Pepper and Mango, she would run along the river trails or sit quietly on rocks daydreaming. She became one of the people maintaining a holding pattern just outside the perimeter of the community.

Waiting. Waiting to get in. Waiting for someone to die or move away. Waiting to have her own little place on this shelf of land above the river. When people weren't home, she would peek in their windows and imagine her things in place of theirs.

Her presence became so substantial that she became a frequent guest at our potlucks, a close friend who was up on all the gossip.

But more than anything else, she was waiting.

We tend to hermit ourselves away more in the wintertime. We miss each other in the winter, locked away as we are. One winter, to try to maintain a social connection through these dark months, we decided to form a book club. Oh yes, and we'll make it also a potluck so we can eat too. Read books together and then create dishes that thematically relate to the book. It was pure genius. Of course, the books became a moot offering. The gatherings became opportunities to eat, laugh, and drink. And that was okay too.

Darcy became part of this club. I think that night we were supposed to be reading *Midnight in the Garden of Good and Evil*. Something about heat and intrigue, so we could escape the cold in our imaginations, at least. On the table at the gathering sat a bottle of wine or two. And a nice pot of Gumbo Z'Herbs, the succulent vegetarian version of the more commonly known and traditional Gumbo. If you haven't tried it, I recommend you do.

Lynne, the woman living in Joe's place, never melded with the matriarchy of the neighborhood. One of the first things she declared upon moving here was that she really didn't like women. We invited her once, and only once, to a potluck. She spent the time insulting many of us and declaring that the only person down here she was comfortable with was Ralph, the old hermit at the end of the road. The political stance of the ruling matriarchy was that Lynne didn't belong and that Darcy did. Like most of the other women of The Crossing, Darcy was fiercely independent, opinionated, and mildly neurotic. Also like the rest of us, she was a fantastic cook.

Join me as I reconstruct that night.

"I just want to live here sooo bad." Darcy has finished her first glass wine and is pouring a second. Darcy becomes quite a different element of woman when combined with wine. The more wine she consumes, the more porous becomes the filter between her emotions and her mouth.

"If only Lynne would leave. She doesn't belong here," Darcy declares, her eyebrows coming together in two calculating slopes. "She muzzles her dog." Her voice eases into the whisper of a conspirator. "She listens to opera."

"Maybe she'll fall into the river," Darcy adds, with a mildly evil twinkle in her eye.

"We can't wish bad things on her," Concetta says. "But maybe we can send her on her way in a good way. Maybe she can find something better somewhere else."

"Then I can move into her house," Darcy mumbles. Her head is sagging a bit from the wine.

Concetta brings forth a voodoo doll. Not the old-fashioned kind whittled from wood that has the enemy's hair attached to its head, but a silly-looking novelty shop voodoo doll. It comes with pins topped with bright red pinheads that can be strategically placed on the doll's body.

"We'll send her away with good thoughts and intentions." We laugh, pouring more wine, and sway about Concetta's wooden kitchen table. Candles burn down. We try to mop up the excess of alcohol in our bellies by picking about the remains of the meal. It is nearing midnight. The perfect hour for spell-making! We're feeling especially bewitching in this sisterhood of overindulgence.

Darcy holds the voodoo doll in her hand. "Lynne, it isn't that we don't like you, although we don't. We don't want bad things to happen to you. We just want you to go away so that I can live in your house," she says, looking down with great sincerity at the voodoo doll. Darcy is childlike and charming as she converses with the little doll. The doll reaches out to her with its rigid stuffed arms. Black-ink eyes beckon. Its O-shaped mouth seems sympathetic.

Darcy takes a pin and shoves it deeply into the doll's head. "You will remember a long-lost lover and move into his house. It's a nice house with a fenced yard. Your dog no longer has to be muzzled."

She sticks another pin into the ear. "You are invited to New York to run a small opera house. You are surrounded by people who love opera just like you do."

Another pin pierces the doll's eye. "You'll see that this place isn't very nice for you. After all, look at how we are sitting here wishing you would leave."

Darcy sticks a pin into the doll's heart. "Oh, but Lynne, that handsome man loves you so much. It's okay for you to go with him and find love and happiness."

"We give you permission to leave," we all chant together. "Go away, Lynne." The candles flicker. The wine pools in the bottoms of glasses. We are suddenly aware of a mysterious breeze rattling the windows of Concetta's small house.

Darcy, like a mystic exhausted from collaborating with the spirits of another world, collapses across the table, her arms spread and her hair draping into a bowl of half-eaten gumbo. The voodoo doll has fallen from her hand.

Concetta picks it up and props it against a half-empty wineglass.

"It will be interesting to see if she's still here when we wake up," she says, and we nod, as if we really believe we have the power to manipulate the forces of the universe.

Darcy is gathered into our arms and brought to my house, where she sleeps off the wine on my sofa.

In the morning, there is no sign that Lynne is packing her bags. We all have mild headaches from the wine. We assuage them with more leftovers.

Spring comes, and when the plants pop free of the frozen earth and the flowers bloom, we seem to bloom too, emerging from our dark homes, rubbing our eyes in the sun. The voodoo night has long passed, and still Lynne is down there at the end of the street.

She doesn't belong here . . . or does she? How can there be any outsiders in this place of outsiders? Aren't all of us outsiders someplace? Maybe she is part of some mysterious feng-shui neighborhood balance. I've never asked her how she found her way down the hill to The Crossing or why she remains. Whatever the case, she's still here, with her muzzled dog and opera music. We accept her, maybe not in a loving embrace, but with what we hope is a dignified maturity, and a promise to keep the voodoo doll tucked away where she belongs.

Darcy has given up on The Crossing and moved to Colorado. She calls every few months to say she misses us, and I tell her that we miss her too. At potlucks we light a candle in her honor: our little ghost resident of The Crossing.

....

Gumbo Z'Herbs

Ingredients

- ¾ cup vegetable oil
- ¾ cup flour
- 1 bell pepper, chopped
- 2 serrano peppers, chopped
- 1 onion, chopped
- 2 celery stalks, chopped
- 4 cloves garlic, chopped
- 2 bay leaves
- 3 tablespoons Cajun seasoning
- 1 tablespoon cayenne powder
- 6 cups vegetable stock (or chicken stock for non-vegetarian version)
- 1 cup chopped okra (fresh or frozen)
- 2 pounds mixed greens – collards, cabbage, mustard, turnip, chard, dandelion, etc.

- 1 tablespoon filé powder or to taste
- Cooked white or brown rice for serving, if desired

The magic of Cajun cooking comes from when the ingredients are mixed with the same passion as the ingredients of our hearts. In this alchemy, our deepest desires simmer patiently to perfection. The roux is the base, that smoky flavor that grounds the whole recipe.

Instructions:

1. Start with the roux: ¼ cup of oil and ¼ cup flour, whisked with a wooden spoon in a deep cast-iron skillet or other heavy pan; keep the heat low and it will slowly darken, and with your patience and enthusiasm, it will deepen to a sultry mahogany color. This will take about 15 minutes. Don't let it burn. If it does, start over.
2. Sauté chopped onions, garlic, and celery into the roux: the holy trinity of soups.
3. After the onions become translucent, add the peppers, two bay leaves, and the vegetable broth. Let this concoction simmer, about 20 minutes.
4. Bravely toss in the okra, the greens, and your seasonings.
   o A note on the greens: the Louisiana tradition is that the more greens you use in this dish, the more friends you will have in the coming year.
5. Serve in bowls over white or brown rice.
6. Sprinkle in filé powder, parsley, and hot sauce to taste.

Oh, a few raised eyebrows, wondering what in the world is filé and where in the world can I find it? Sassafras is its other name. That's the source of filé. Basically a dried weed used in southern cooking. It can be hard to find. If you can't, well, you'll miss out, not experiencing its pungent little kick, but the gumbo will still be gumbo, and you will deeply satisfied with your tourist venture into the land of the Voodoo kings and queens.

CHAPTER 7

LOVE ME LIKE A ROCK:
Buddha Smiles

The fireplace mantel in Gus's house resembles a Valentine's card. A collection of Baroque-style ceramic angels prance, play harps, sing, and gaze off, love-struck. "I fantasize a lot," Gus says coyly, corners of his mouth turning upward just a bit, as he cocks his head slightly to the side. It seems appropriate that he should live in the house he does, the old ferry runner's house built in 1890. I imagine that, like the ferry runner, Gus spends hours gazing upon the river, watching birds and dreaming.

He has crafted this house from its original 25′ × 25′ square foot structure into something more reminiscent of a small castle, with fantasies wrought from solid elements of stone and wood. It's preposterously large for a single man, but that was not the intention. Gus once had a wife and it was to be a family home, where meals were cooked and shared, where they could observe their child growing: sweet baby, lively toddler, spry child, awkward adolescent, and finally, proud young man. It was a house full of possibilities, like their relationship, like the baby growing in Abbey's belly even at the moment of their marriage.

You know you are entering a fantasy as soon as you approach the house and are greeted by the Celtic Green Man, whose face adorns an impressive knocker on Gus's massive wooden front door. Behind this door are now 3,000 square feet where Gus's fantasy was to evolve. Hand-sanded and varnished wood floors play out into a puzzle of rooms.

Gus's living room is cozy, with a fireplace and its angel-laden mantel and antique furnishings. Five ornate stained-glass light fixtures dangle pendant-style from the ceiling.

Throughout the house stand multiple Buddha statues and other Asian artifacts representing holy and wise men, including a very old figure of a wise and hunched Dymio crafted in Japan in the 1920s, and another of China's Laozi.

About sixteen hand-woven wool oriental rugs, magic carpets from the Far East, though purchased on eBay, are scattered about the floor. Gus points out the uneven patterns. "Most likely they were made by children just learning the craft from their elders."

There are playrooms for his son Shawn, a well-stocked pantry off the kitchen, efficient-looking offices, bedrooms, two staircases, and even a turret built onto the second floor that Gus uses as a meditation room.

Gus is a man with a raging need to build and construct that drives him deep into the nights, with his hammer finding nails and his saw finding wood. He sets his mind to a task others would find daunting. His determination causes all to stand from his way as he forges his fantasy into reality.

We hear his saws deep into the night, but in spite of these Herculean efforts, each room resists being finished. Its beauty is interrupted by half-painted walls and exposed beams. In his dining room, green paint spreads toward the center of a south-facing wall and then stops, so brushstrokes fade, leaving a white starburst in the center. There are places where the old wooden studs are exposed and tufts of soft pink insulation peek from between two-by-fours.

One room, however, is without flaw. It is the elegant bedroom on the first floor, reserved for Gus's mother. He wants her to have a place where she can be comfortable when she visits. It is furnished with a grand Civil War–era walnut bed frame, covered in a green floral spread, with matching throw pillows with silk tassels. A large bay window reveals a view of the river below, waves belting against the rocks.

On the outside of the house, Gus has built steps out of black basalt carved by Baltic stonecutters from Chinook's earlier days. Gus tells me he has seen a picture of this stonecutter standing with a proud, protruding chest, positioned next to Teddy Roosevelt in front of the newly constructed Chinook High School.

"Stones make me feel good," Gus says. "I discovered this climbing in Joshua Tree National Park as a med student, struggling with the stress of that situation." A variety of stones he has collected are scattered about his yard. One is a large chunk of granite that weighs ten tons. He had it hauled into the neighborhood from across the river. I, and others in the neighborhood, believed this immense stone was a Valentine's or birthday gift to his then wife, Abbey.

No, Gus explains. It's his rock. He brought that in because he saw it at a construction site. He points a partial finger (he cut the top off accidentally while sawing at the same time that he was arguing with Abbey) to a set of narrow white condominiums built on the south side of the river. He brings his hand back down and pats the granite. "I just like stones."

"This is the one that I got for Abbey." It is a smaller, soft-shaped piece of quartz, with a pinkish hue and ripples of white foam markings. It sits on the ground about twenty feet from the ten tons of granite. The quartz he found in the woods sixty miles north of Chinook. "It was a relationship gift. I don't think she ever understood or valued it."

The quartz is beautiful, but it's the granite and its massiveness that captures the imagination. Gus dug a hole three and a half feet into the ground to lodge the granite in place and planted it upright so it stood nearly seven feet into the air. But Abbey didn't trust the stone looming so high above their small son as he played outside. She was terrified that it would fall on him.

The word at The Crossroads was that Abbey and Gus fought, often, and about almost everything: the manner in which the house was constructed, the manner in which affection was or was not expressed, who was caring for Shawn, and especially about the granite stone. It became the center point of a brutal tug-of-war.

"Abbey was my fantasy. But as the Dalai Lama said, 'The sex is good, but then the trouble begins.'"

Gus and Abbey's relationship ended after two stormy years in which Gus brought the concept of family into the construction project. Before Abbey packed her bags and left, Gus took a bulldozer and pushed the massive granite stone prone. Now, when Shawn visits, he climbs about it and uses it as a back wall for his forts. In winter, if the temperature drops low enough, Shawn and Gus arrange a spray hose above the stone so that water sprays and drips, then freezes. A thick sheet forms on the stone's flat top, while ribbed columns drape its sides and clusters of mushroom-shaped bumps emerge from random water drops. It is a beautiful combination of the elements of water and stone.

In The Crossing of the nine houses, only one seems to hold a couple successfully cohabiting. Lisa and John's twelve-year marriage is a beacon of possibility. Other houses are filled with loners, many of us with long histories of tumultuous relationships and poor matches.

Gus wonders about all this. Is it the self-absorbed fascination we have with our journeys, or our extreme eccentricities that make us so unable to couple successfully?

Gus looks out his picture window to the water roaring beneath, water that could carry any of us away and beyond, despite whatever hands we may attempt to grasp.

"Perhaps," Gus sighs, "there is just too much water."

Buddha's Smile

A dish to cleanse and nourish the soul.
An adaptation of Buddha's Delight.

- 4 tablespoons cooking oil
- 4 Napa cabbage leaves
- Oyster mushrooms, cut into pieces – about 3 cups
- 1 package marinated and grilled tofu, sliced
- 3 slices fresh ginger
- 3 tablespoons hoisin sauce
- 3 tablespoons soy sauce
- 1/2 cup water
- ½ cup cashew nuts
- Hot chili sauce or paste, to taste
- One 3½-ounce package thin rice vermicelli noodles; soak 20 minutes in lukewarm water

In a wok or large fry skillet, heat oil; stir fry mushrooms and ginger for 2 minutes; add cabbage leaves. Continue stirring until cabbage is just wilted. Add liquids and cellophane noodles. Cover and cook for 5 minutes or until noodles are translucent. Gently toss in grilled tofu and cashew nuts.

CHAPTER 8

MILO'S PANCAKES OF GREAT SUSTENANCE

Chinook was the city of my father, Milo's, childhood. I had heard of it only through stories. It formed the backdrop of his adventures in youth. That was during the Depression years, when he and my Grandpa Frank pulled handcarts of fresh vegetables from the Valley to sell at the outskirts of the city center.

My father first brought me to Chinook for a visit when I was fourteen. He promised that before we left, he'd buy me a Coney Island at a downtown café. First, he had to visit an old childhood friend named Don Riddle who lived someplace called The Crossing.

I remember him driving across a bridge over a very impressive river. Enormous rocks jutted through the surface and sent the water into turmoil. Then a paved but broken road curved through a desolate landscape.

Another dirt road seemed to dive down and into another world. There were strange crumbling houses clinging to the edge of the river. Every tree seemed to want nothing more than to grow, and to reach out and expand and twist around whatever it was growing near: another tree, an old building, a wooden fence. Their roots bullied their way through the neighborhood's old sidewalks.

Don Riddle was a stinky, old, fat man who lived in a broken-down, box-like house. He had a skinny wife, a sad woman who never seemed to leave the kitchen, where she fussed over meals for her always hungry and impossibly cranky husband.

I escaped outside as soon as possible. Just south of Don's little house was about a half-acre of nothing but rubbish. Don, you see, spent most of his days collecting whatever he could that was free and bringing it back to his home in The Crossing.

There was no one to be seen in the neighborhood. I wondered who lived in all those curious houses, thrown like a handful of seeds on this small shelf of land above the river. When I came back as an adult and moved into the neighborhood, I discovered what a menace Don and his rubbish were to the neighborhood. Eventually, however, Don became too debilitated to function. He sold his property and abandoned his treasures. Gus eventually came to possess much of Don's former land and spent weeks piling the rubbish into giant green dumpsters rented from the city. In all, 80,000 pounds of trash collected over decades were removed from the land. This is the space where Doctor Gus later erected his granite.

It was always an odd coincidence that the first place I came to on my first visit to Chinook was The Crossing, to visit miserly old Don Riddle, my father's childhood friend. So my father is yet another of the legendary ghosts of The Crossing, and I want to share a bit about him.

On Sunday mornings, in another small town many miles from here, my father would get up early to begin the complicated process of making pancakes. He assembled me and my two sisters, still wearing our pajamas, along the kitchen counter and equipped us with an assortment of kitchen tools: spatulas, eggbeaters, and forks. Already bacon was frying in a cast-iron skillet, because bacon grease was an essential ingredient in the pancakes. An assortment of flour sacks knelt against one another along the counter. Eggshells were scattered about with their broken edges up, gently rocking on their rounded bottoms.

The pancakes were a hardy mix of flours, grease, eggs, and milk. Father lorded proudly over the assemblage process. Measuring was taboo in our family, so the act of dumping flour into the mixing bowls in the correct proportions and quantities was solemn work. My father inspected the quality of our batter, lifting it gently with a spoon. Slowly, he turned the spoon sideways, so the batter slid in a thin stream back into the bowl. Whether our mixing instrument was a fork or an eggbeater, we counted to at least ten before we stopped mixing. The batter was made thin, so each cake was delicate, in contrast to the heavy ingredients.

I remember how my father tested the heat of the grill by placing butter on its surface. If the butter sizzled, it was time to ladle the batter onto the grill.

My father was greatly indulgent in his love, and these pancake-making sessions were one of the many expressions of his affection. He introduced us to his friends as "the three most beautiful daughters in the world." We each had funny pet names: Little Lamb, Skunk, and Cabbage. One birthday, he bought me not one stuffed animal, but an entire menagerie. My room was filled with animals and looked more like a toy store than a bedroom.

Best of all, my father made us pancakes on Sunday mornings. My sisters and I stood around him in amazement as he poured the perfectly consistent batter onto the grill. Some mornings he would feel extra playful and would skillfully form people adorned with hats and scarves, an art form requiring patience and imagination.

He created complete families that transformed into a deep brown before our eyes. Sometimes he formed pancakes to look like our pets, and then dogs romped and horses galloped across the grill.

Yet my father was simply not able to love consistently. He had a dark side that would take him unpredictably and painfully away from us. Sometimes for days or even weeks, we would not know where he was. He would return with fragmented stories and a bruised face. He was a man who drank, and his drinking brought him trouble. As he got older, he forgot our birthdays, forgot to make pancakes on Sundays, and eventually he forgot his way home. He died in Chinook, returning to his childhood home where once he and the miserly Don Riddle were children and played together. Before my thirtieth birthday, my father left us for the great and unknown beyond.

It's the father of my early childhood whom I hold in my heart and who lives, in spirit, among us in The Crossing: the man who made pancakes of great love and sustenance. As if he knew he needed to give us something to carry us through times less abundant.

Milo's Pancakes of Great Love and Sustenance

Ingredients-- Measurements provided as guideposts only.

- 1 cup white flour
- ½ cup buckwheat flour
- ½ cup rye flour
- ¼ cup cornmeal
- 1 teaspoon baking powder
- ½ teaspoon baking soda
- ¼ cup any combination of oil, butter, and bacon grease
- 2 eggs
- 1½ cups milk
- 1 tablespoon molasses
- ¼ cup honey
- 2 teaspoons vanilla

Instructions:

1. Fluff dry ingredients.
2. Beat wet ingredients together.
3. Fold into dry ingredients.
4. Stroke 10 times or until just mixed. Check batter consistency. It should run slowly from a spoon. If it is too thick, add water.
5. Use ½ cup batter per pancake.
6. Grill on hot, butter-coated grill. Flip when bubbles form on top. Both sides should be a deep brown.

CHAPTER 9

THE RED SOFA:
Meals to Cook Over an Open Fire

The Flats serve as our moat. The area above us boasts the highest crime rate in the city. Meth houses abound; children run loose and reckless about its streets.

We pass through there daily to get to the "outside world," and often our "neighbors" come down to The Crossing, too. They come with enormous Rottweilers heaving against their chains, or sometimes strolling casually and unleashed with their owners. The children of The Flats ride bikes down to our neighborhood to get to a favorite swimming hole. I call them the Potty-Mouth Brigade because they know more dirty words than I do and call them out frequently in loud child voices. Still, they are only children. We've bandaged their legs when they have fallen off their bicycles, hugged them when they cried after finding a dead dog in the bushes, and pretended not to notice when we've looked out our windows and saw them stealing fruit from our trees.

Sometimes those from The Flats steal other things from us, like lawn mowers, papers with our personal identification information from our mailboxes, and once a car belonging to one of our beloved teenagers, Brook. It was an inexpensive little Toyota circa late eighties with a little hula dancer on the dash that swayed with the movement of the car. Brook and Concetta drove up and down the streets of The Flats looking for the car with the little hula dancer. When they found it, policemen had surrounded the little blue car and had the thief and his girlfriend in handcuffs. The thieves had spent the whole day joyriding. The car was returned, hula dancer and all.

People dump garbage in the grassy area above our neighborhood: big piles of discarded furniture, automobiles, and children's toys. These discarded items reek of lives in disharmony. "Pigs!" we yell at the piles of garbage as we drive by.

There is a particular railroad underpass that, when we drive beneath it, we cross ourselves. It possesses an eerie, evil feeling. We sense that horrible things have happened in its dark shadows. Often cars are parked here, engines running, lights off, their passengers apparently engaged in activities they don't want the world to witness.

Once, in early summer, someone dragged a big red sofa down the tremendously steep embankment from The Flats to the river. I jogged by there each morning, and there was new drama every day. First, there were the revelers: a group of about five large, tattooed men sitting on the big red sofa, a big bonfire flaming in front of them, drinking beer and playing '70s hard rock music on a boom box. They partied down on the banks for three days. Some homeless teens moved in next. They slept there at night and disappeared during the day.

We all got together and decided to haul this sofa away from the river. This would require packing it an eighth of a mile down a very narrow trail and into The Crossing, where it could be loaded onto a truck and taken to the dump.

I went down to see the sofa after work one day, knowing the sofa evacuation project had been planned and was to be executed the next day. But now someone had put the sofa halfway into the river, and it was waterlogged. Now it was way too heavy to carry!

The next day, the sofa was gone. Someone had pushed it into the water, and the current carried it away. At the end of summer, while picking blackberries four miles downriver, I found its battered remains scattered about the shore.

I sat on a log for a while just thinking about its journey to this place. All the while, the river's current sang to me sweetly. Inside me, bones shifted. I think to myself, "That's not me. It's a red sofa."

We may not want to think it could happen to us. Our fear of losing our ability to pay bills, our sanity, the organized appearance of our utility drawer. But sometimes you have to admit that there is a freedom that comes with it, too.

My Papa Milo rode the rails during the Depression. Those were hard times. He made what he called "Hobo Stew" over an open fire. In my childhood, he'd recreate this dish for us (on a stove) and tell stories about this reckless, frightening adventure, when he and Don Riddle, at the age of fourteen, roamed about the U.S. searching for work. You could tell that despite what must have surely been a harrowing time, he kind of dug it.

Maybe that's one of the reasons some of us are drawn to camping. It gives an opportunity to temporarily remove ourselves from the many responsibilities of the civilized world. Something about watching a fire, shivering a little in the night air, cooking our food in a manner similar to the way our distant ancestors did thousands of years before. It's an opportunity to contemplate all you have to be grateful for. Sing a song immortalized by Janis Joplin about having "nothing left to lose." Cook a good hot meal. Invite some friends to join you.

However, when you're had your fill, I recommend you get your butt back home where it's safe and comfortable and your responsibilities await. Ultimately, there is no utopian freedom— just a different set of strings to attach yourself to. Don't be lured into this sad enchantment. None of us really want to be the red sofa floating down a river in spring.

Lasagna Cooked Over Hot Coals

I've cooked a lot of food over open fires or coals.
This vegetable lasagna is a pleaser.

- 1 package no-boil lasagna noodles
- 15 ounces full-fat ricotta cheese
- 1 egg
- 2 cups shredded cheese mix
  - I like a mix of cheddar and mozzarella
- 2 cups fresh baby spinach
- 28-ounce jar of your favorite pasta sauce
- Cooking oil
- A Dutch oven or cast-iron pan with a good lid.
- About 30 hot coals and a prepared fire pit.**

**Dirt, cement, or stone foundation, surrounded by rocks and far away
from grasses, shrubs, or other flammable items. The key is to surround
the pan with heat so the lasagna cooks evenly.

Instructions:

1. Use a Dutch oven or heavy cast-iron pan with a good top. Heavily oil the sides and bottom to prevent sticking.
2. Begin with one cup of sauce, followed by a layer of lasagna noodles. Spread a layer of the egg and ricotta mixture.
3. Add another 1/2 cup of sauce, followed by 1 cup of fresh spinach and 1/3 of the cheese. Continue to layer until all ingredients are gone, ending with sauce and cheese.
4. If cooking over coals, use 10 hot coals to create a bed for your Dutch oven. Once the lid is secured over your assembled lasagna, place another 18–20 coals on top of your Dutch oven. (One option is to turn the lid upside-down and fill the center of the lid with coals.)
5. Cook for 30–40 minutes. Cooking time will vary depending upon how hot your coals are. You'll know it's done when the sauce is bubbling, and cheese is melted. You can also cook these in a Big Green Egg or other BBQ. This is a simple recipe, but the Dutch oven and the use of fire make it exceptionally delicious.

"HOBO STEW"

My dad cooked this in a tin can when he was riding the rails during the Depression. I recommend using a foil packet. (Thank you, modern conveniences.)

Use your own favorite vegetables. Here are some possibilities:

- Onions
- Garlic
- Baby carrots
- Corn
- Peas
- Green beans
- Mushrooms
- Cherry tomatoes
- Baby potatoes
- Cut sweet potatoes

Favorite seasonings

- Olive oil
- Fresh rosemary
- Fresh parsley
- Ketchup
- A splash of soy sauce
- Optional: precooked hamburger or sliced summer sausage

Instructions:

1. Cut up vegetables into bite-sized pieces.
2. Place on an 8-inch sheet of aluminum foil. Place 1 cup of mixed vegetables on the center of the foil; add a small amount of precooked hamburger.
3. You can put the aluminum foil into a small bowl to create a nice form for your vegetables or do it freestyle.
4. Fold sides of the aluminum foil into the center and fold securely to create a strong "seam."
5. You can put this directly into the coals or on a BBQ, or place it on a baking sheet and cook in the oven. It is done in about 30 minutes, when vegetables are tender.

CHAPTER 10

PRECIOUS ONES:
Moon and Sun and Star Cookies

Children are all precious. You cannot bring a child into your life without having every part of your soul rearranged and transformed. Triplets, well, they multiply that effect.

Nathan, Cody, and Tanner are special mischief-makers. Even though biologically they belong to Hank and Morgan, they really belong to The Crossing. They are our little fairies who jump, giggling, from trees to shatter the seriousness of our lives.

Morgan and Hank were in their early forties when they decided to start a family. They were thinking maybe one child, so it was a bit of a startle to find that three spirits were forming in Morgan's womb. There was much fussing to do over Morgan, who had temporarily traded in her career as an architect to be this amazing incubator. Her body kept getting bigger and bigger and bigger and bigger. When she walked down The Crossing, we peered out our windows in amazement at the immense bubble forming on her front side. Her belly was much larger than the rest of her body, so she looked like a pipe cleaner with a big grapefruit attached to it.

Days before the triplets were born, I was watching her from my kitchen window as she wandered in her backyard. She was dressed in one of those special black pregnancy leotards that covered her body in one piece of fabric. Walking slowly, she gazed off toward the river. She stood for several moments, swaying softly. Then something on the ground caught her eye. She bent down awkwardly to retrieve the item. She seemed so precarious in her state that I held my breath, knowing that if she fell . . . oh my gosh! I didn't want to think about it. She carefully brought herself back up to standing and held a tiny leaf up to the sun. Before the week ended, the boys had arrived.

Nathan, Cody, and Tanner were big noisy babies who cried at what seemed like orchestrated intervals in a plan intended to drive their parents deep into the clutches of madness. At The Crossing, there was much head-shaking and sighing. How were they surviving? Pre-triplets, Hank and Morgan had lived this rather idealistic, intellectual, and adventurous life: traveling, kayaking rivers, pursuing fancy, high-paying careers in architecture and engineering.

Their pre-triplets house could have been a Pottery Barn showcase. Wooden shelves and black-and-white landscape photos were arranged in perfect symmetry on freshly painted peach-colored walls. Tasteful cream-colored linen drapes slid open to reveal the expansive river scene behind their dining nook. Expensive upholstered chairs fell in line around a glass coffee table. On this coffee table was a hand-carved, elongated wooden tray lined down the center with hand-dipped Marion Berry scented candles.

The triplets, in a mighty tornado of energy and personality, quickly disrupted everything for Hank and Morgan. Within two years, the picture window overlooking the river had been repeatedly broken and replaced. After the fourth time, they just covered it with cardboard. Crayon scribbles covered the once peach-colored walls. Chairs with torn upholstery now served as building foundations for rambling forts, constructed with a combination of plastic climbing apparatuses and blankets. Their house had become a wreck.

The triplets grew into know-it-all, mischievous toddlers who were quick to hug. Each had a unique personality. Tanner had a tender spirit and his feelings were easily injured. Nathan was more engineering and precise of mind. Cody, the clown, started young playing practical jokes.

It was fun to watch Morgan and Hank chasing after the wild boys. And we were soooo glad it wasn't us!

One day I was out on the deck entertaining a mishmash of guests: my son Marcus and his girlfriend, my sister from the Coast, old friends, and maybe a lover or a past lover. I really can't remember now. Back and forth I went from my house to my deck, carrying platters of Greek food: baba ghanoush, kabobs, pasta, and olives. It was one of those late summer evenings when the air was still and warm, but not too hot, and filled with the smells of leaves and flowers.

Let's visit the scene. Hank is calling Cody. This is common. The triplets are getting quite quick on their feet. It's hard to keep track of them. I continue carrying the meal to the deck. A bottle of wine and eight wine glasses. Don't forget the napkins.

Hank is still calling for Cody. His voice is beginning to rise, reaching that point of panic. I look over and see him bounding about the yard, looking behind shrubs and down over the bank toward the river that, although low in the summer, is still a force to be considered with respect.

I deposit my last load of food dishes and abandon my guests. Soon, word has spread. Cody can't be found! A toddler hunt begins. We spread out through the neighborhood. We look in everyone's yards, cars, inside and even under houses. Our eyes scan the river as we conjure up but refuse to name the worst of possible scenarios. And then remember, with a terrible sense of foreboding, the transient who had wandered through earlier in the evening. Had our safe haven been breached?

Had we become too comfortable? Had tragedy slipped in while we were busy toasting friends, weeding our gardens, or making a to-do list for the next day?

Hank had been watching the children, just him—Morgan was at

a yoga class. It was simply a very big job for one person. Turn your back for a moment . . .

We are now standing all in a circle in the triplets' living room, surrounded by a chaos of toys. Hank takes Nathan by the shoulders. "Nathan, where is your brother? Where's Cody?"

Hank's hands are shaking, his face flushed in terror. Nathan puts one hand sheepishly over his mouth to hide a grin and points to a cupboard in the corner of the room. Hank goes there and pulls the door open. Out tumbles Cody, all giggles and smiles.

Hank sits in the middle of the floor and sobs; his shoulders convulse, and big tears stream down his face. Tanner, as always the sensitive one, comes and gives him a hug.

We all cry, too. We all have our precious ones. We had to expand our hearts so wide to hold our love for them. Imagine how we would fall deep into sad, echoing chambers if a precious one were lost.

As a little boy, my son would sit on the kitchen counter when I was baking cookies. With spoon in hand, he was the master of measuring. It was his job to make sure that four equal cups of flour made their journey to the mixing bowl. Immersed in the process, he seemed an essential component of the recipe; dusted with flour, he often looked like he could actually be an ingredient.

When my son entered my world, it was like a magnolia bud blossoming in my heart. It was truly a shift in my ability to give and receive that mysterious and omnipotent feeling defined by the word "love." I had never felt so full. To make sure he knew the depth of my love for him, I would often repeat, "I love you more than the moon and the sun and stars." I made it into a wee nursing rhyme and comforted him with it when, exhausted from a day of play, he would cry against my shoulder until my cooing words eased him into dreamland.

Hush now sweet darling. Hush now, don't cry.
The angels in heaven will sing you a lullaby.
And the dream fairies are waiting to bring on your dreams,
Of riding white horses and other great things.

I love you more than the moon, and the sun, and the stars.
With your sparkling eyes and mischievous grin,
I love you just the way you are.
Toes clean or toes smelly, dry nose or runny,
Near or far, wherever you are,
I love you more than the moon and the sun and the stars.

So hush now sweet darling. Hush now, don't cry.
The angels in heaven will sing you a lullaby!

These cookies honor him and all precious ones in our lives.
Perhaps today it a perfect day to bake some Moon and Sun and
Star Cookies to present to your beloved. And remember the simple
incantation: "I love you more than the moon and the sun and the
stars." Its magic is unequaled.

Moon and Sun and Star Sugar Cookies

Ingredients-- Makes about 60 cookies
- Moon-, sun-, and star-shaped cookie cutters
- ¾ cup unsalted butter, softened
- 1 teaspoon vanilla
- 1 cup sugar
- 2 eggs, room temperature
- 1 teaspoon baking powder
- ⅛ teaspoon salt
- 2½ cups all-purpose flour

Instructions:
1. Cream butter and sugar in a bowl with an electric mixer until smooth. Add eggs and vanilla extract. Blend well.
2. In a separate bowl, mix flour, baking powder, and salt.
3. Stir flour mixture into butter and sugar mixture until just mixed; do not overmix. Form into a ball. Place each ball of dough between pieces of floured parchment paper.
4. Using a rolling pin, roll out the dough through the parchment paper to about ¼ inch thick.
5. Place rolled dough on a cookie sheet and place in the refrigerator for at least one hour, but preferably overnight.
6. When ready to finish cookies, preheat oven to 400 degrees F. Place another sheet of parchment paper on cookie sheets.
7. Take the dough out of the refrigerator. Remove the top sheet of parchment. You may need to smooth out the dough with a rolling pin once more and add another dusting of flour if the dough gets sticky.
8. Cut the dough using the cookie cutters. Place the figures on the parchment paper–covered cookie sheet. Bake cookies for 5–7 minutes, until just brown.
9. Carefully place cookies on a cooling rack until cool. I like to keep them simple and unadorned, and just give a light sprinkle of sugar when they are still warm. But this could be because I don't have much of a sweet tooth. You can certainly use your favorite frosting or glaze to fancy them up. Enjoy!

Chapter 11

A MEAN SOUTHERN WOMAN:
Dishes to Stir up Memories

The night my mother had her stroke, I was on my deck overlooking the river, entertaining an assortment of people: my friend Julie; my son, Marcus, and his girlfriend, Trish; and my new partner, Sam. It was one of those lovely late-summer evenings when people could still wear short sleeves and not be chilled. I had baked a whole chicken in the juice of fresh tomatoes, with green olives, lots of garlic, and fresh oregano from my garden. The chardonnay was chilled and buttery.

Then the phone rang. I heard my mom's gargled, panicked voice. It sounded like she was speaking with a mouth full of Jell-O.

"I've had a stroke, Debbie Rae. I'm in the hospital." I stood silent, looking out the window at the giant trees that grew in the yard. I could hear the voices from my dinner party drifting through the screen door of the kitchen and, more distant, the sound of the river, moving low and slow across the rocks.

I realized that she couldn't be too bad or she wouldn't have been able to talk and explain what had happened. My second thought was more selfish. I knew that everything I had buried of my childhood—the random corporal punishments and the embarrassment at having a mean Southern mother—had found their way to me like a slow-moving train at night. I heard that train building speed just outside my door, waiting for me to get back on board.

Self-preservation is an interesting process. As is denial. I didn't respond like a good daughter. I rationalized that her boyfriend, Bill, was there, besides which my sister was on the way.
I had guests.
I went back down to the deck, gulped down the last of my glass of wine, and then poured another. Now people were leaving. I was short with my partner. "I can't deal with this tonight," I said, not telling him why I was so exasperated with him for asking if we could move up into the house. He was always complaining that he was cold when no one else was.

When my friend Julie loaded up her car, I asked if she would drop me off at the hospital on her way home.

My sister and my mom's boyfriend were gathered about my mom. I realized I was drunk. My father would have dealt with a family crisis by getting drunk, too. The tree. The fruit.

It was too early to know how much Mom would recover. She could talk, although the Southern accent she had successfully hidden for decades came back. The stroke had mostly affected her right side, and that side of her face drooped strongly, and her right arm and leg were paralyzed. Her coordination was nonexistent.

Her day had been quite dramatic. Mom and her live-in boyfriend, Bill, had been out on their five-acre plot of land, in their little trailer with a yard full of animals: peacocks, dogs, chickens, cats. She had felt it coming while standing in the kitchen and had tried to make it to the phone. A retired nurse, she knew immediately that it was a stroke. It hit harder just as she grabbed the phone. She went down to the floor, pulling the phone out of the wall as she fell. "Bill," she whispered. But Bill, he was hard of hearing. Her whispers dissolved in the air, unnoticed. She had been a care provider for Bill through the past few years as he became increasingly unable to tend to his daily care. He was a crotchety old ass, in my opinion. I hated that he always yelled at my mom: "Make me a sandwich!" or "I need another Pepsi!" Never a please or thank you. Now it was his turn to see to her in this moment of need, but he couldn't hear her call.

Eventually, he sensed something was wrong and hobbled on his arthritic feet and knobby legs into the kitchen. I can see him kneeling slowly to her. Yelling, as he always did, "Irene? Irene?" He could have plugged the phone back in and called 911, but that's not what he did. Instead, he got in his big red Cadillac and drove to the neighbor's house three miles away. The neighbor, named Velvet, was the kind of hard woman you sometimes find living in the woods, a former drug addict who had bought a trailer on the same dirt road Mom and Bill lived on. She wanted, I suppose, to distance herself from her former associates to better stay clean. They could have called 911 from her house. A helicopter could have come from the city and been to the trailer in 10 minutes, but they didn't call.

Together, this 86-year-old crippled man and a 60-year-old former addict half-dragged, half-carried my mom into the car and drove her 55 miles into the city. Not to the closest hospital, on the north side of the city, but instead all the way through downtown and up the south hill to the hospital farthest away from Mom's and Bill's trailer in the woods.

Mom arrived at the hospital four hours after she had her stroke. It sounds like I'm being judgmental, but I really can't, can I? As the daughter who sat on her deck for an hour drinking wine after receiving the phone call that her mother had had a stroke. No, I really can't judge.

Before Mom had her stroke, I preferred to refer to her as my mother, rather than Mom. I liked how it recognized the biological reality of our relationship without implying a lot more.

It wasn't that I had totally separated myself from Mom. It's more like I kept her attached to a very thin string that I could use to lead myself from the city and follow it back to that trailer in the woods, the same trailer where I had lived in my tiny room so many years ago.

It had not been a safe home, and I hadn't had a safe or nurturing childhood. My father, when he was around, was usually drunk. He was the kind of father who would give you $20 to shop while he went to a bar, but if you woke him when he was still half drunk, he could erupt in a rage. As I've mentioned, my mother was a nurse. She took drugs from dead patients to take herself. She liked to work nights, so she took uppers before she went to work and Valium when she got home, spending the day stretched out in her robe on the coach, dosing with her hair in rollers. My two older sisters looked after me until they left home. After that, I had to mostly fend for myself. I survived. Left home for college. Met a man. Had a baby. My mother accused me of "rising above my raising." It wasn't a compliment.

The distance I put between myself and Mom was for self-preservation. It was not that I didn't have feelings for my mom. Oh boy did I have feelings, strong feelings: bitterness, rage, distrust; but cushioned always between these aching emotions was a bit of pure and simple love. We were family. I couldn't turn my back.

About once a month or so, I followed that invisible string to the trailer, where I would sit for about an hour, listening to Mom bitch about everyone who had taken advantage of her, to her complaints about the crazy people who were her neighbors, and to her regular despairing remarks about whichever one of her children was currently disfavored. My son came with me. He loved playing with her menagerie of animals. She loved cooking for him a bounty of Southern foods: fried chicken, grits, biscuits, and for dessert, deep-fried maple bars.

Now my mom was in a hospital bed. I wondered if I loved her enough to make sure she was taken care of. She had been a good grandmother to Marcus. She adored and spoiled him, and he loved her dearly. If for no other reason than this, I would do my best.

Mom had listed me as her emergency contact and administer of her financial and legal matters. Doctors called me to update me on her status. "We'll be moving her to St. Joseph's Care Center at 10:00 A.M. Wednesday." The nurse talked to me as if I was a good daughter, as if I would come and pack my mother's things and accompany her on this move. And so, I did.

"I know it's hard to see your mother like this," she said sympathetically, nodding her head, touching my shoulder.

I was thinking about how much more of this I had to tend to. I wanted to get back to my work, to my life, to cooking dinner for my son and our friends, and snuggling with my lover to watch indie films. When would this detour end?
"Well, she's not going to die right away," I thought cynically to myself, "so you may as well settle into tending to the things you have to tend to."

Mom looked so sad and lonely. The new "stroke" version of her didn't lecture me or complain and insult people. In fact, she was pleasant. She called all her medical helpers "dear." She patted my back softly when I gave her a hug. I started coming in a couple times a week to help her eat her meals.

I realized I didn't really know my mom, not this version anyway. "Oh, they've stopped mashing up your green beans." I raised a spoon to her mouth and slid a spoonful of French-cut green beans into her mouth. "That must be nice."

"I'm not choking so much. They upgraded me." She would make jokes to the staff. She named her bad arm Charlie. "I named him Charlie because he's just like a man. Useless." The attendants chuckled and patted her. With the attention, a little-girl smile, crooked from her stroke, warmed her face.

It was like a little bit of innocence had slipped back into her life.

Her husband sat with her all day long and kissed her goodnight when he had to leave to go to the assisted living home where he was now living. Everyone oohed and awwed at their affection. It *was* sweet, until on occasion he would yell at Mom and tell her she wasn't trying hard enough to get better and throw pillows at her. Love had always been complicated for Mom.

Mom moved into a new stage then, with a myriad of doctor's appointments, physical and occupational therapy. My sister, Rose, helped me get Mom to them when she could. My other sister, Penny, lived too far away to come except for once every few months.

It was a lot.

Three years later and she was in an assisted living home. Her husband had died the year before, and she had a new boyfriend. My sisters and I were frustrated by her phone calls, how she continued on about getting her own house. "I want to tell her fine, go ahead, if that what you want, go and do it. If you can do it on your own, then just go and do it. Stop talking about it," Penny complained to me over the phone.

One day when I went to visit her, I found her in her bed watching the Mariners game. She didn't look at me but began talking straightaway.

"Lynn, the therapist, asked me today why I hold on so tight when I'm sitting on the therapy table. 'You look like you're scared,' he said to me. I told him when I was six years old, I rode in the back of a flat-bed truck 80 miles from Big-B to Mobile. It was night and there wasn't anything to hold on to but the wood of the truck bed. There was no railing or anything. I was afraid I was going to fall off, so I held on real tight. We were going to the hospital to see my Papa, but he was already dead when I got there."

Mom was still looking at the TV. I patted her hand sympathetically. "I'm so sorry. That sounds like you must have been really scared, and sad too."

"I was." She still hadn't moved her eyes from the TV. I had never heard that story before. I knew that her childhood was hard, and that her mother, Miss Kate, who wouldn't let anyone even call her Grandma, was considered to be crazy and fanatically religious. She burned Mom's magazines and wouldn't let her or her siblings listen to the radio or play games. I knew my mom's childhood was filled with hard work. But I had never heard my mom talk about it with so much vulnerability.

To counter Mom's sadness, I decided to encourage her to say positive things to herself. I knew that people who had traumatic childhoods never feel they have their basic needs met. I told my mother that whenever she felt troubled to say, "I am safe. I am loved. I am a beautiful child of God." I wasn't particularly religious, but Mom was starting to attend church services, so I felt that the God reference was important to add.

When she first started this little mantra, she couldn't get through it all. It came out as more of a stuttering rant: "I … I … I am safe. I … I … I am safe …. I am safe…." I helped my mother practice the mantra every time I saw her and over the phone when I called her.

She began reciting it to the nurses, her therapist, and everyone who visited her. They told her what a great saying it was and that they were going to start saying it themselves.

Mother began telling more stories, in her straightforward, droll manner. Whenever a new story was revealed, she would repeat it to several people, and then, it was as if her mind had chewed on it enough. She would stop telling that story and move on to another. Sometimes she told funny stories. They made her giggle mischievously like a young girl.

She joined a group that gathered weekly to work on their autobiographies. One day I saw the scribbled notes on a yellow pad: "When I was 12, I was hurt by some men." I turned my eyes away. She saw me, and said firmly, "Just put those over there."

She was telling her story. She was healing. Just when we think it's all winding down our best work has just begun.

Mom and I moved into this place of reconciliation, which sometimes felt like I was leaning against a jagged cliff, rocks poking me in the back. Sometimes it felt like a free fall through darkness. Just when you think the anger will never let you go, a lightness fills your heart. These moments felt like slipping into the warmest bed and snuggling with a sweet puppy. Now I found myself saying, "I am safe. I am loved."

Here, I surrender, in this place where grace lives and breathes, dances and sings and sometimes even giggles like a schoolgirl yet to know the world's sorrows.

Recipes from a mean and tender Southern woman

Southern Fried Chicken

- 2 cups buttermilk
- 2 large eggs
- 3 cups all-purpose flour
- 2 tablespoons salt
- 2 teaspoons black pepper
- 1 tablespoon paprika
- 4 pounds bone-in skin-on chicken pieces—keep in mind dark meat will cook faster, so fry dark and white meat in separate batches.
- Crisco vegetable shortening for frying

Instructions:

1. In a medium bowl, combine the milk and eggs. Whisk to blend well.
2. In a 1-gallon Ziplock bag, combine the flour, 2 tablespoons salt, and pepper. Seal and shake to combine.
3. Dip the chicken pieces in the milk and egg mixture and let excess drip off into the bowl. Set already dipped pieces aside on a plate until you have three or four.
4. Add the dipped chicken pieces to the bag of seasoned flour.
5. Seal the bag and shake well to coat the chicken pieces thoroughly.
6. Remove to a plate and repeat with the remaining chicken pieces.
7. Heat the oil in a deep, heavy skillet to 350 degrees F.
8. Fry the chicken in small batches (3–4 pieces) for about 10 minutes on each side, until golden brown and thoroughly cooked. Only cook a few pieces at a time. Make sure the pieces are not crowded against each other.
9. When cooked, place on a paper towel–lined plate. Repeat until all pieces are cooked. Keep fried chicken warm by placing it on a rack and pan in a 150-degree F oven.

Cheesy Grits

- 3 cups vegetable broth
- ½ teaspoon salt
- 1 cup quick-cooking grits
- ¾ cup shredded cheddar cheese

- ½ teaspoon hot sauce
- 1 small can chopped green chilies

Instructions:

1. Bring broth and salt to a boil in a two-quart saucepan.
2. Add grits and reduce heat to low. Continue cooking for 10 minutes or until thickened.
3. Add cheddar cheese, hot sauce, and green chilies. Simmer another two minutes.

Vegetarian Southern-Style Green Beans

- 1 cup sliced baby bella mushrooms (to replace bacon)
- 1 tablespoon soy sauce
- 1 tablespoon maple syrup
- 1 medium onion, finely chopped
- 2 cloves garlic, minced
- 2 lbs. fresh green beans, trimmed
- 3 cups vegetable broth
- 3 tablespoons butter
- Salt and pepper to taste

Instructions:

1. Sauté the baby bella mushrooms in 1 tablespoon butter over medium heat until just softened. (Use the same pan you will use to cook your beans.) Remove from pan.
2. Next, toss the sautéed mushrooms with the maple syrup and soy sauce. Then place the mushrooms in one layer in a small baking dish and broil until crisp.
3. In the same pan used for sautéing the mushrooms, add another tablespoon and sauté onions and garlic until translucent. Add the green beans and vegetable broth.
4. Bring to a soft boil and reduce heat to a simmer.
5. Cover and let simmer softly for one hour. Strain. Add remaining butter, the crispy mushrooms, and salt and pepper to taste.

Chapter 12

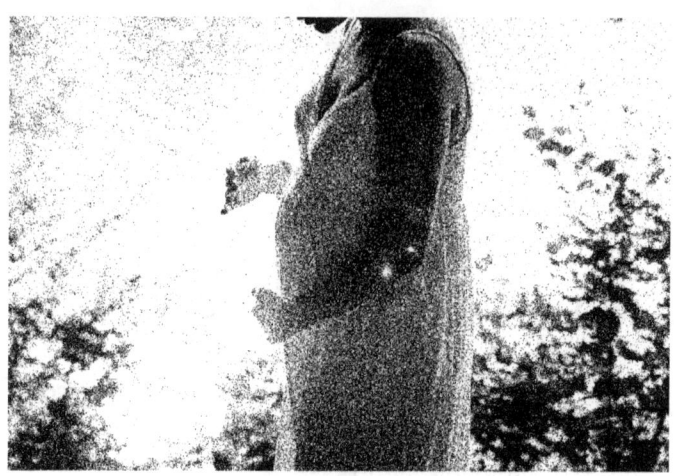

BITTER WITH THE SWEET:
An Unforgettable Chocolate Cake!

Every day, Leonard takes a stroll through The Crossing. Not by himself, but steadied by his mother, Lisa, or his Aunt Lydia, or his caregiver, Allen. His arms and legs are spindly and cannot support his weight. His large head with its freckled face hangs absently off to one side. Leonard has been living in this world for nearly twenty-five years, and his body has grown longer and bigger as the years have passed. But in his head, they say, are the thoughts of a child of only a few months. What is in his heart and soul is a mystery.

Lisa is not with Leonard's father anymore. She has a new life now, taking care of this precious grown son, her new husband, and her other children now nearing their teens. It's a quiet life they live in The Crossing.

Lisa is a small woman with fine blonde hair and narrow wrists. Leonard is a good foot taller than Lisa. When she walks with him, she wraps an arm around his waist and lets his body lean against her. He doesn't have a vocabulary. Cannot enunciate words. Cannot express whether he enjoys these daily walks or finds them a chore.

Still waters run deep. That is what I think of when I see Lisa. Her face is calm. I've never seen her lose her temper.

It is not the life she originally envisioned for herself. Through her twenties, she lived with Barry, Leonard's father. They lived that "art-style" life. She was a potter and he a writer and a charmer. They traveled and lived in other countries. She taught pottery, patiently demonstrating how to pull the wet clay up from the spinning pottery disk as it danced and wobbled to finally find its form. A vase. A cup. Maybe a bowl, blooming from its base like a flower. Barry taught philosophy, his words floating through the air, kissing and nibbling at the young ears of his students. Then in a cabin in the mountains of Washington. Barry needed the solitude for his writing. In the evenings they gathered with other creative types: writers, artists, sculptors. They discussed ideas while sipping beer and wine. It was a life where choices were made around the noble idea of the elusive creative. How to best bolster their mutual desire to live the authentic life of the artist, far from the rigid demands of the systems and corporations.

Barry was not a classically handsome man so much as dramatic, with a tall, bulky form. He was prematurely bald, with chocolate-drop eyes and a nose that swooped down and back up to form a small ball at the tip. He knew it took more charisma and balls then talent to reach the type of notoriety he longed for. His formula proved successful.

Lisa and Barry came to The Crossing in 1974. They bought a little house down the road from Lisa's cousin Lydia. It was a small, working-class house, with no frills and little space. Lisa made pottery in the basement. They poked a hole in the ceiling to raise it up high enough so that Barry could stand up without bumping his head.

Lisa wanted to be an art teacher, but she settled on a job as a substitute teacher at a school for the severely developmentally disabled.

Barry liked women a lot, and this marred their marriage the way an open-pit mine does the earth. Lisa had a cure for Barry's straying eyes. She got pregnant. Like so many women, she believed the myth that a new baby would make things better. Pregnancy was a happy time for them, full of promises and the shared dreams of watching a little child grow.

Lisa's labor was so intense she hallucinated. After 48 hours, the doctor finally used forceps to rip Leonard from her tiny frame. Unfortunately, this happened too late. Although they didn't know it at his birth, Leonard had been deprived of oxygen. For a few months Lisa enjoyed being a new mom to a beautiful fat baby with tufts of brown hair.

Then the seizures began and Lisa noticed a certain dullness to her sweet baby's eyes. Barry saw Leonard as a reflection on him. The baby looked like him, but this version of him slobbered and drooled and shook and made odd, primitive noises. It was more than Barry could stand, so he left Leonard to Lisa's care and went on to write poems and novels in which he explored from afar the despair and drama of his child's brokenness.

We all have these opportunities to revise ourselves. Some come softly. Some come in deep nights of labor and blood. Lisa had a calling that ran more deeply through her than all her artist yearnings and God-given talent. It was through tending to her child and all his fragments that Lisa discovered her grace. She went back to school to obtain a degree in special education. Now, her days in a classroom are filled with those who have challenges similar to those faced by her son. Teens who still wear diapers. Young people, blessed with brilliant minds, but whose nervous systems are unable to fulfill the expected communication processes needing for walking, eating, talking. Big-bodied humans who open their mouths and speak with the innocence of a toddler. Lisa's days are filled with this amazing array, variations from expectations. Like the potter that she is, she takes the raw essence of their being, as if it were clay, and she lets their form be revealed in the unique and unstandardized form. After all, in pottery, sometimes the most interesting vessels are the ones whose forms are irregular, even misshapen.

As the years passed and Leonard grew to be a young child, a new man came. Two more children arrived, two beautiful, healthy children with the kind and loyal husband whom Lisa married.

Life continued.

After a full day with her "irregular vessels" at her work, Lisa comes home to her husband and the two children they share. She also comes home to Leonard, this mysterious vessel of humanity who is her son. She feeds him. She lets him swing from a specially designed chair that hangs in a room off the kitchen of their now expansive, remodeled home. On spring, summer, and fall weekends, she takes him for walks through The Crossing. Dogs come out to greet them. Leonard moves his head about, perhaps taking in the colors of the flowers blooming in people's yards, enjoying the white clouds scuttering across a blue sky, or listening to the whimsical chatter of the birds.

Twenty-five years after his dramatic entrance into the world, he lives his simple life in his home on the river, No one knows what happens or doesn't happen in his brain, his heart, or his spirit.

"Life takes you where it wants to take you and gives you the lessons you need to learn," Lisa says without elaboration or self-pity, but with the diligence of a woman who knows the purest love is unconditional and can take you places you never imagined you could go.

Bittersweet Chocolate Cake

Ingredients
- 1 cup unsalted butter, removing one tablespoon to use for buttering the pan
- 8 ounces bittersweet chocolate, such as Lindt, broken
- 1 cup sugar
- 4 large eggs, lightly beaten
- ½ teaspoon instant coffee granules. I use Café Bustelo, but any instant coffee will do.
- ½ teaspoon kosher salt
- ¼ cup all-purpose flour, plus extra for the pan
- Sweetened whipped cream or vanilla ice cream

- 1 tablespoon confectioners' sugar for sprinkling on top of cake when baked
- Fresh strawberries, sliced and sprinkled with sugar

Instructions:

1. Preheat the oven to 350 degrees F. Butter and flour an 8-inch springform pan.
2. Place a large heatproof bowl over a pot of simmering water, making sure the water doesn't touch the bowl. Put the butter and chocolate in the bowl, stirring occasionally, until the chocolate melts. Take the bowl off the heat and set aside.
3. First, whisk the sugar into the chocolate mixture; then whisk in the eggs, coffee, and salt, whisking until the mixture is combined and smooth. Sprinkle on the flour and fold it in with a rubber spatula until it's incorporated.
4. Pour the batter into the prepared pan and place it on a sheet pan. Bake for 30 to 40 minutes, until the cake doesn't wobble when you jiggle the pan and the top is slightly cracked.
5. Remove from the oven and cool completely on a baking rack. The cake will deflate as it cools. Run a small knife around the cake and remove the sides of the pan. Use a tight-meshed sieve to distribute confectioners' sugar on the top.
6. Cut the cake in wedges and serve warm or at room temperature with sweetened whipped cream or vanilla ice cream. Add a tablespoon of sliced, sugared raspberries.

CHAPTER 13

THE HEROIC ACTS OF JUBILEE:
Dishes to Celebrate Fido

Our dog Jubilee would lie on the front porch when I traveled, waiting, watching, protecting our home. Our house was big, so I had a roommate who fed and cared for Jubilee while I was gone. My son, an older teen then, had his own car and navigated between his dad's house and mine, mostly staying at his dad's when I was away, coming over to pick up fresh clothes and to visit Jubilee.

When I was a child growing up on a farm, our dogs were a big part of our lives, but it was a different time and we treated them differently. Dogs slept outside on the porch. They ate the cheapest dog food and occasional table scraps.

Jubilee and I are the continuation of a domestication and be-friending process that began 30,000 years ago. One of my favorite cartoons shows a pack of wolves looking at a human settlement in one panel, and one wolf saying to another, "They have food. What could go wrong?" The next panel shows a poodle dressed up in little bows and a sweater.

Jubilee was not a dog who would tolerate bows or sweaters. She loved the woods. Together, we ran the river path. Her eyes were wolf-like. Barely domesticated, she bit into the tender neck of a small chipmunk that ran across her path, then tossed it indifferently to the side of the dirt path and continued on her way. Predator is what predator does.

She was a great huntress and protector. I felt safe with her vigilant eyes and ears watching out for us. Our bond was as tightly braided as any.

On one of my runs, she had looped off to hunt. I was coming down a steep dirt hill that ran from the upper bluff down to the river. It was a dry, hot summer day, and the smell of pine needles baking in the sun filled the air. I stopped midway down to watch a pair of ospreys play on the air currents.

A movement at the bottom of the hill caught my eye. I looked down to see a man hiding behind a pine tree, staring at me. I froze. My mind began calculating where I could run to quickly, where it was less desolate and I wouldn't be so vulnerable. The man stood between me and the trail back to The Crossing. In the opposite direction, the trail dead-ended at the river, its strong currents white-capping over the rocks. Behind me was a straight-up slope to the top of the bluff, where a few houses were scattered. Could I outrun him? He started wiggling his finger, as if beckoning me to come down the slope, while his other hand slid down toward his groin.

At the top of my lungs I yelled, "Jubilee! Jubilee!"

Within moments a streak of black dog, like a shadowy bolt, came dashing down the hill and toward the man behind the tree. He began running, scared witless, Jubilee at his heels.
Don't mess with anyone in Jubilee's pack.

One hot summer day, I, Marcus, and several of the neighbors grabbed air mattresses and inner tubes for a cool float down the river. In late summer, the river, while still wide, quiets sweetly, moving at a near sloth pace, except where the old bridge used to hang. The big boulders there create rapids that require a small amount of skill and a good dose of courage to meander through. We were near the rapids when I realized that Jubilee had been following us along the trail and now, as we got near this gurgling portion of the river, she was trying to swim out to meet us. She was nervous for us, and we were nervous for her. She was nearly ten years old now and the years were slowing her down. I could see her struggling in the current. I tried, but was unable to paddle to her on my air mattress. Fortunately, she managed to get back to shore and continued down the path. When I made it to shore myself, I found her trembling in the shrubs. She whined in that heart-wrenching way dogs do when they are deeply heartbroken and in true despair.

Sadly, the fight in the rapids took her down a notch. She was a bit weaker after that.

We exchanged evening runs for walks. Her right leg was becoming arthritic, tightening up her hips so her walk was hobbled and stiff. Frankly, I was getting older and slowing down a bit, too. We were still sympatico. On one of these evening walks, I saw Jubilee look behind us, a wary look in her eyes. I turned to see that we were being stalked by three coyotes, who obviously sensed Jubilee's more weakened physicality. I imagined they had been watching that proud she-dog for years as she bounded over the river trails and were thinking it would be great sport to take her down.

Oh, but it was time for me to repay all the protection she had given me over the years. Angrily, I stomped toward those grizzled grey beasts, yelling and waving my hands. Damned if they were going to get to my Jubilee! They turned tail and ran back into the brush. I patted Jubilee's black head reassuringly.
Jubilee lived to be sixteen years. Until the week of her death, we continued to walk, although toward the end it was just a slow walk to the end of the street. It was a ritual we both treasured.

She had never been a furniture dog. She preferred to lie on the floor, or better yet, outside, where she could keep watch over The Crossing. Because she had that heavy coat of black fur, this preference was just fine with me. However, in her later years, I realized she had a little secret—a private decadence she enjoyed when no one was home. I started catching her jumping off the sofa when I walked in the door. Her loss of hearing prevented her from hearing my car pull into the driveway. Hmmm! That explained all those black hairs on the furniture over the years.

It was a sad day when she passed. Marcus and I buried her in a hand-dug hole in the back yard under a wild rose bush. So, this is another tale of a great spirit passing. In life, loss is how time is marked. The pursuing tears are how our love is measured.

The older I get, the more spoiled my dogs are.

My new dog, little Ellie, stretches her 95-pound body between me and my partner like a deer, legs sprawling everywhere. She delights in chasing balls and having doggy playdates. A fawn-colored rescue, she's a wonder whose breed we don't know and don't care about.

Curled up against her, there is pure sweetness. I feel like I'm getting an endorphin IV drip. Sleep on the porch? I don't think so. When she turned one, she had a birthday party. The neighborhood dogs attended. She received presents and shared her birthday cake with her doggy playmates. Yes, I've become one of those people.
Some people might say it's a bit extreme. I do not care. If we all are "going to the dogs," we will be better for it. With their enthusiasm for small gestures, they remind us that we do not have to be great to be wonderful, nor handsome to be beautiful. How can we possibly give them the love they deserve in the short time we are blessed with them?

This chapter is for all the good Fidos in the world. Yummy recipes for dogs. Bon appétit! Translated to doggy language: Ruff! Ruff!

Happily Going to the Dogs Recipes

<u>Note</u>: These recipes use only healthy ingredients. However, they are meant to be treats and should be given only in moderation. If your dog is overweight or has any health issues, please consult your veterinarian before feeding any of these treats. Portion size will vary in accordance with your dog's size and weight. Most of these will make multiple servings.

Spaghetti with Meatballs

- Whole wheat spaghetti- cooked according to package directions
- 1–2 tablespoons of olive oil for drizzling and for baking pan
- ½ lb. ground beef
- 1 egg
- 1–2 tablespoons shredded parmesan cheese

Instructions:

1. Cook whole wheat spaghetti according to package directions. When finished, use a knife to cut spaghetti into one-inch pieces and drizzle with olive oil.
2. In a small bowl, mix the ground beef with the egg and shape into bite-sized balls. Place the small meatballs in a glass baking pan that is greased with olive oil.
3. Bake at 375 degrees F for 15 minutes.
4. Let noodles and meatballs cool completely. Serve meatballs over the oiled noodles with a sprinkling of parmesan cheese.

Meatloaf

- 1 lb ground beef
- 1 egg
- ¼ cup shredded carrots
- ¼ cup quick rolled oats
- 3 tablespoons tomato paste (make sure there is no sugar or salt added)

Instructions:

1. Mix all ingredients except the tomato paste.
2. Form into a loaf and place in a loaf pan, greased with olive oil. Spread tomato paste on the top.
3. Bake at 350 degrees F for 45 minutes.
4. I like to bake sliced, unseasoned sweet potatoes with the meatloaf as a nice accompaniment. Cool completely before serving.

Ground Turkey, Green Bean, Sweet Potato, and Brown Rice Casserole

- 1 lb ground turkey
- ¼ cup chopped frozen green beans
- One sweet potato, peeled and cubed
- 1 cup cooked brown rice

Instructions:

1. Mix raw turkey with frozen green beans, cubed sweet potatoes, and cooked rice.
2. Bake in an oiled casserole dish (I always use olive oil because it's good for dogs) at 350 degrees F for 30 minutes or until there is no longer pink showing in the turkey meat and the sweet potato can be pierced easily with a fork.
3. Cool completely before serving.

Peanut and Banana Frozen Yogurt

- 2 cups plain Greek yogurt
- 2 tablespoon xylitol-free peanut butter
- 1 medium banana

Instructions:

Mix ingredients in a food processor. Pour into a mold or ice-cube trays. Freeze for 2 hours. Yummy!

Doggy Birthday Cake

- 1 cup whole wheat flour
- 1 teaspoon baking soda
- 2 tablespoons vegetable oil
- ¼ cup xylitol-free peanut butter
- ½ cup plain applesauce
- ½ cup pumpkin puree

- ½ cup shredded carrots
- 3 tablespoons milk
- 1 egg

Frosting

- 1 cup plain Greek yogurt
- ½ cup xylitol-free peanut butter
- Dog treats for garnish optional

Instructions:

1. Preheat oven to 350 degrees F.
2. In a large bowl, combine flour and baking soda.
3. In a second bowl, combine oil, peanut butter, applesauce, pumpkin puree and egg. Stir until combined.
4. Blend dry ingredients into the wet.
5. Pour mixture into a greased, round, 8 inch baking pan.
6. Bake for 25 minutes.
7. Once cooled, add yogurt frosting and optional dog treat garnishes.

CHAPTER 14

WHAT FUTURE COMES:
Drinks that Inspire Sitting and Daydreaming

In early spring, the surveyors came to the open meadow where the river bends. This is the place where High Bridge used to be, just west of The Crossing. When Lydia first moved here, High Bridge, the abandoned railroad bridge, still stretched high above the river. She walked across it once, standing a hundred or so feet above the water just upstream from where Logan Creek meets the river water. It must have been something to stand up on the bridge and look out to the rough edges of Chinook, with downtown in the distance, the tops of pine and deciduous trees scattered about the landscape. Only wild sage and prairie grass held back the sandy hillside trying to ease toward the river. The sandy bank was broken by clusters of boulders. The Chinook River was wide and especially wild at this place.

Now, over thirty years after they tore down High Bridge, the city is building another bridge. They're calling it Stevenson's Bridge, after one of the developers who has been attempting to take over much of the river property for years. The new bridge will be a "walking" pedestrian bridge and will connect pieces of the city's pedestrian trail. Soon, people will be able to walk or ride their bikes uninterrupted all the way from the city of Holden (forty miles east), through downtown, and miles past Bolder Park, the geographical wonder about seven miles downriver from us, where the river creates dangerous swirls around enormous basalt rocks.

The residents of The Crossing watch in nervous anticipation. Change is coming. In later fall, bulldozers begin carving a road out of the hillside. Next, concrete pillars are erected in the water. Workers are there each day by seven A.M., working diligently, pouring cement and building pilings.

By spring it is finished. It seems all of Chinook comes out to walk across the bridge. Of course, they found our river trail. Each weekend, walkers in warm spring jackets, wrapped in scarves and wearing hats, come purposely through our neighborhood on their way to and from the new bridge. They are like modern Lewis and Clarks, exploring our private, simple little neighborhood as if it were the last frontier. It's not one or two people, but crowds of eight or ten. The dogs are going mad with it. They bark constantly, so disrupted are they by these intruders.

The taxes have gone sky-high. Suddenly, now that the bridge has been built, we have value. We must pay the city for our increased status. A new developer with a sinister-sounding name, Black Rock, has purchased the desolate land between The Crossing and The Flats. They're talking shopping centers and condominiums. We feel the hot breath of yuppies on our necks as they covet our riverfront property.

The Crossing will not budge. The folks here will not give up our homes to this gentrification. The road will remain unpaved; yards and gardens will continue overgrown and houses unconventional. Dogs will not go on leashes or be fenced in backyards. Tethered dogs don't smile on Sunday mornings.

So, if you happen to turn down the little street and find yourself in The Crossing, you might receive a wave or an offer to join in a meal and a glass of wine. Oh, there will be smiles and chitchat for a while, but don't think it's an invitation to stay for long. Don't bother asking if any of the houses are for sale. They're not. Maybe someone will eventually die and their children will sell their home for a good profit, but we are a healthy bunch, so don't hold your breath.

Now we've shared all that we care to. There are children and lovers to tend. There is art to create, houses to remodel, projects to pretend to complete, sorrows to cry over, gossip and jokes to share, and potlucks to plan. The people of The Crossing have our own little dreams that we dream when we wake each morning. It's time to get back to them.

Special Beverages for Sitting and Daydreaming

Sangria, Spicy Chocolate Chai, Black Cherry Spritzer with Cognac, Mulled White Wine

Sangria

- 1 bottle of dry red wine, such as merlot
- 1 cup brandy
- 2 oranges, peeled and separated
- 2 lemons, sliced into wedges
- 1 cup chopped pineapple
- 2 cups pineapple juice
- 3 cups sparkling water
- 4 cups ice

Mix ingredients and serve in a large punch bowl or pitcher.

Chai

- 6 black teabags
- 6 cups water
- 1 cup milk
- ¼ cup sugar
- 1 teaspoon cinnamon
- 1 teaspoon cardamom
- 1 teaspoon clove
- 2 teaspoons vanilla
- ⅛ teaspoon dry hot chili powder
- 2 tablespoons unsweetened chocolate cocoa

Simmer water and teabags for 5 minutes. Remove teabags. Add milk, sugar, and spices. Gently simmer for another minute before serving.

Mulled White Wine

- 2 (750 ml) bottles of dry white wine
- 2 oranges, sliced into rounds
- ½ cup brandy (optional)
- ¼ cup honey
- 16 whole cloves
- 4 cinnamon sticks
- 4 star anise

- Garnish with an orange slice, cinnamon sticks, and star anise

Combine all ingredients in a non-aluminum saucepan and bring to a simmer over medium heat. DO NOT BOIL—it will remove the alcohol. Reduce heat to low and let the wine simmer for at least 15 minutes or up to 3 hours. Strain, and serve warm with garnishes.

Black Cherry Spritzer with Cognac
Per Serving

- 1 cup seltzer
- ¼ cup black cherry juice
- 1 slice of lime
- Shot of cognac, if desired. Omit for a refreshing nonalcoholic beverage.

CHAPTER 15

POT-LUCKING FOOLS!
Dishes to Share with Friends, Family, and People You Barely Tolerate

In The Crossing, we love to gather and share food. We have had spring celebrations that included a maypole. The children dressed up and attached wings to their backs to dance around like butterflies and fireflies. When Morgan was about to give birth to the triplets, we had a big cooking party. All the women came together and prepared a dish Morgan could freeze and cook up during the postnatal exhaustion. We have spring barbeques, summer Sangria fiestas, fall picnics, birthday bashes, Christmas soup parties, and evenings celebrating Buddha's enlightenment. The process of cooking is what intrigues me: the act of invention, the smells, the tastes, the colors, the texture of dried spices crumbling between my fingers. But mostly I, and my neighbors, love to cook because we like to fill the bellies of the people that we love. We want them to be comforted and fattened.

Potlucks are wonderful: the wild tumble of food coming together. People nibbling, gossiping, stealing recipes.

It is also quite wonderful to get up on Sunday and cook a full breakfast of egg dishes and breads, cheese, and fresh fruits to feed sleepy people in pajamas and underwear. In other words, life is always better accompanied by good food and loved ones.

Meals, I like to serve with certain aplomb. Stay out of my kitchen. Gather in another room. Don't look at my dirty dishes piled precariously in the sink, sauces dripping off the counter and onto the floor. Let me carry it piled high on platters and present this to you as if it came about through magic.

Cooking, for me, is a passionate and personal journey. As is true for many people, certain dishes call forth my past and my family's history. My mother's Southern flair, my father's Minnesota French. Vegetables parade throughout, as I grew up on a farm and outside our back door there was always a vegetable garden. What follows are some recipes from The Crossing, many of which have been shared at our many gatherings and potlucks.

Pot-lucking Recipes

Curried Deviled Eggs, Spinach and Feta Cups, Smoked Salmon and Artichoke Dip, Summer Pasta Salad, Asian Noodle Salad, Stuffed Chicken Thighs, Katharine Hepburn Inspired Brownies

Curried Deviled Eggs

- 6 eggs
- ¼ cup mayonnaise
- 1 tablespoon stone-ground mustard
- 1 teaspoon curry powder
- ½ teaspoon dried parsley
- 1 tablespoon sweet apple cider vinegar
- ¼ teaspoon ground black pepper
- Slices of green olives stuffed with pimentos to garnish each finished egg half.
- 1 pinch paprika for garnish

Instructions:

1. Place the eggs into a saucepan in a single layer and fill with water to cover the eggs by 1 inch.
2. Cover the saucepan and bring the water to a boil over high heat.
3. Remove from the heat and let the eggs stand in the hot water for 15 minutes.
4. Drain. Cool the eggs under cold running water. Peel once cold.
5. Halve the eggs lengthwise and scoop the yolks into a bowl. Mash the yolks with a fork. Stir the mayonnaise, mustard, curry powder, parsley, apple cider vinegar, and pepper into the egg yolks until combined, spoon into the egg white halves.
6. Garnish with paprika and a slice of green olive. Chill before serving.

Spinach and Feta Cups

- Nonstick vegetable spray
- 1 package puff pastry sheets, thawed in the refrigerator (Can substitute pre-made pastry shells.)
- 1 egg beaten
- ¾ cup Ricotta Cheese
- 1 (6 ounce) container crumbled Feta Cheese

- ½ cup freshly grated Parmesan cheese
- 1 (10 ounce) package frozen chopped spinach, thawed and drained
- 2 cloves garlic, minced
- 2 tablespoon minced sun-dried tomatoes
- 1 tablespoon finely chopped dill weed
- ¼ teaspoon ground black pepper
- Paprika

Instructions:

1. Preheat the oven to 375 degrees F. Spray cups of a 12-cup muffin pans) with nonstick cooking spray.
2. Roll out the thawed but cold puff pastry sheet on a lightly floured surface into a rectangle using a rolling pin.
3. Cut into 12(approximately 3 1/2-inch) squares using a pizza cutter. Lightly press puff pastry squares into each cup of the muffin pan and prick with the tines of a fork.
4. Mix the beaten egg into the Ricotta Cheese. Add feta cheese, Parmesan cheese, spinach, sun-dried tomato, garlic, dill and pepper together in a bowl.
5. Spoon cheese-spinach mixture evenly into the cups, being careful not to overflow the cups. Sprinkle with paprika.
6. Bake in the preheated oven until the pastry is puffed and the corners are golden brown, about 15 minutes.
7. Cool five minutes before serving.

Smoked Salmon and Artichoke Dip

- 4 oz smoked salmon
- 8 oz package cream cheese, softened to room temperature
- ¼ cup mayonnaise
- ¼ cup sour cream
- 1 teaspoon Dijon mustard
- 1 teaspoon lemon juice
- ½ teaspoon chopped dill
- 2 tablespoons chopped chive
- ½ cup artichoke hearts, drained and chopped
- 1/2 cup parmesan cheese
- Salt and pepper
- Parsley or additional chives for garnish

Instructions:

1. Preheat oven to 375 degrees F.
2. Blend cream cheese, sour cream and mayonnaise in a food processor or use a hand mixer to blend until smooth.
3. Fold in mustard and lemon juice. Stir in dill, chives and artichoke hearts, parmesan cheese, salt and pepper.
4. Transfer to a glass baking dish and bake for 20 minutes until hot and gooey.
5. Garnish with parsley or chives. Serve with artisan bread slices or your favorite crackers.

Summer Pasta Salad

- 1 16-oz package corkscrew pasta, multi-colored, cooked and cooled
- 2 cups spring greens
- 1 sliced cucumber
- 2 green onions, finely chopped
- 1 large beef-steak tomato chopped
- ¼ cup carrots matchstick cut
- ½ cup sliced kalamata olives
- ½ cup shredded parmesan cheese

For dressing

- ¼ cup olive oil
- 1 tablespoon mayonnaise
- 2 tablespoons red wine vinegar
- 2 tablespoons fresh lemon juice
- ¼ cup olive oil
- 1 tablespoon minced garlic
- ½ teaspoon Dijon mustard
- 1 teaspoon honey
- ¼ cup mixed summer herbs – basil, oregano, thyme
- Salt and pepper to taste

Instructions:

1. Mix cooked pasta with summer greens, cucumber, tomato, green onions and carrot matchsticks and olives.
2. Whisk dressing ingredients in a small bowl. Drizzle over noodles and vegetables.
3. Add shredded parmesan. Stir. Chill before serving.

Asian Noodle Salad

- 8 oz package Chinese style noodles – cooked and cooled
- ½ cup carrots, thinly sliced
- 3 green onions, diced
- 1 cup bean sprouts
- 1 package marinated tofu, such as teriyaki
- ¼ cup crushed peanuts
- for dressing:
- 1 tablespoon vegetable oil
- 2 garlic cloves, finely diced
- ¼ cup coconut milk
- 2 tablespoons peanut butter
- 2 tablespoons fish sauce
- 1 tablespoon brown sugar
- ¼ cup olive oil

- ¼ cup fresh cilantro, finely chopped
- ½ teaspoon red pepper flakes
- Juice of two limes

Instructions:

1. Mix noodles, vegetables, and tofu into a large serving bowl.
2. Heat vegetable oil in a saucepan.
3. Add garlic cloves and sauté for one minute.
4. Add coconut milk, peanut butter, fish sauce and brown sugar. Simmer, stirring to keep from sticking, until sauce thickens.
5. Remove from heat. Allow to cool to room temperature.
6. Add olive oil, cilantro and lime juice. Toss dressing gently into noodles. Top with crushed peanuts, red pepper flakes and additional cilantro.

Stuffed Chicken Thighs

- 8 chicken thighs, boneless, skins on.

- 4 tablespoons mixed fresh herbs, such as oregano, parsley, and basil, finely chopped.
- 1/2 cup shredded mozzarella cheese
- 2 beaten eggs
- 1/4 cup milk
- 1 cup Italian herb dried breadcrumbs
- Salt, pepper and paprika to taste.
- Parchment paper
- Toothpicks

Instructions:

1. Preheat oven to 375 F. Line a cookie sheet with parchment paper.
2. In a medium sized bowl, mix cheese and chopped herbs.
3. In another medium sized bowl, whisk eggs and milk together.
4. On a plate, spread the dried breadcrumbs.
5. Open the thigh so the skin is facing down. Place 1 tablespoon of cheese filling in the center of each thigh. Roll or folk thigh so filling is enclosed in the thigh.
6. Carefully holding the thigh together using fingers or tongs, depending upon how clean you want to keep your hands. Though in my experience, fingers work better.

7. Dip the chicken thighs in the egg and milk mixture, then lay on the plate of dried breadcrumbs, gently flipping to assure the breadcrumbs have thoroughly coated both sides of the chicken thighs. Place on cookie sheet lined with parchment paper. Repeat with all thighs, placing them at least an inch apart.
8. Sprinkle with salt, pepper and paprika to taste. Paprika will also give the thighs a nice color.
9. Use toothpicks to keep thighs from opening.
10. Bake in the oven for 20-25 minutes. Let rest 5 minutes before serving.

Katharine Hepburn Inspired Brownies

I've added chocolate chips to this already decadent variation of Katharine Hepburn's famous brownie recipe.

- ½ cup cocoa
- ½ cup butter
- 2 eggs
- 1 cup sugar
- ¼ cup flour
- 1 cup chopped walnuts
- 1 cup dark chocolate chips
- 1 teaspoon vanilla
- Pinch of salt

Instructions:
1. Heat oven to 325 degrees F.
2. Melt butter in saucepan with cocoa and stir until smooth. Remove from heat and allow to cool for a few minutes, then transfer to a large bowl.
3. Whisk in eggs, one at a time. Stir in vanilla.
4. In a separate bowl, combine sugar, flour, nuts and salt. Add to the cocoa-butter mixture. Stir until just combined.
5. Pour into a greased 8 x 8-inch-square pan. Bake 30 minutes.

Dog Smiling Sunday Morning

ABOUT THE AUTHOR

Growing up in a small town in Washington State, my hero was Pippy Longstocking. I was enchanted with adventures. My family was a bit scrappy, so I had to learn at a very young age to be self-sufficient. By the age of nine, I could make homemade tomato soup, grill my own sandwiches, and bake a cake. As a young adult, I explored cooking as if it were the most interesting of adventures. I would go to restaurants and use my taste buds to sleuth out the ingredients. The next evening, I'd attempt to recreate the dish. I also explored the culinary traditions of the world through cooking. It was fun. It probably helped ignite my other great passion -- travel.

I hope you enjoy my adventures in cooking and community. Cooking and sharing food makes life so much sweeter.

Debbie now resides in St. Petersburg, Florida with her partner, Roger, and their dog, Ellie.

www.ingramcontent.com/pod-product-compliance
Lightning Source LLC
Chambersburg PA
CBHW061702120626
46550CB00003B/1051